THE COMMUNITY OF INTERPRETERS

On the Hermeneutics
of Nature and the Bible
in the American Philosophical Tradition

Studies in American Biblical Hermeneutics 3

THE COMMUNITY
OF INTERPRETERS

*On the Hermeneutics
of Nature and the Bible
in the American Philosophical Tradition*

by
R O B E R T   S .   C O R R I N G T O N

MERCER

ISBN 0-86554-284-8

The paper used in this publication meets
the minimum requirements of American National Standard
for Information Sciences—Permanence of Paper
for Printed Library Materials, ANSI Z39.48-1984

Library of Congress Cataloging-in-Publication Data
Corrington, Robert S., 1950–
The community of interpreters.

(Studies in American biblical hermeneutics ; 3)
Includes index.
1. Hermeneutics—History.   2. Philosophy of Nature
History.   3. Bible—Criticism, interpretation, etc.—
History.   I. Title.   II. Series.
BD241.C644   1987   121'.68   87-24807
ISBN 0-86554-284-8 (alk. paper)

·CONTENTS·

Dedicated to
JUSTUS BUCHLER
in friendship and respect

·EDITOR'S PREFACE·

Robert Corrington addresses the topic of American biblical hermeneutics from the standpoint of the thought of the American philosophers
Josiah Royce and Charles Peirce. It is one of the rare studies that attempts
to build a bridge between biblical studies and philosophy, a way of going
about biblical studies that is neglected or ignored by most. Yet Corrington does this in an interesting way that has important methodological
consequences for biblical studies in general, and specific insights into
American biblical hermeneutics in particular.

The importance of Corrington's book lies primarily in the new theoretical grounding it gives the interpretive task, a grounding that draws
upon American intellectual traditions. He rightly approaches the question of an American biblical hermeneutics in the context of the dominant
Continental approaches associated with the Heideggerian school. In distinction to them, he opens up a third interpretive avenue alongside Continental phenomenology and the more literal anti-Continental approach
of such literary critics as E. D. Hirsch. More specifically, a strong case can
be made that with a characteristically reflexive and dependent reading of
the Bible constructed upon the shoulders of such Continental thinkers as
Heidegger and Gadamer, American biblical interpretation has fallen victim to one of two extremes: (1) a pro-Continental approach that is hopelessly open-ended, resulting in an interpretive schematic lost in a sea of
provisional readings claiming equal justification; and (2) an expressly
counter-Continental methodology that takes the opposite extreme of a
literalism rejecting any but the "one authoritative interpretation." While
this latter approach is a matter of concern that lies outside the primary
area of discussion within Corrington's specific work, it is a subject very
much at the center of issues addressed by the Studies in American Biblical Hermeneutics series. Furthermore, it is an issue that is given new
significance by what he has to say. Building upon the interpretive theory
of Peirce and Royce, Corrington successfully builds a hermeneutical ar-

gument that finds a mediating position between these two major contending positions in contemporary America. This is the major reason I see Corrington's book as not only a major contribution to the Studies in American Biblical Hermeneutics series, but a programmatic one as well.

Specifically, this work establishes a third alternative to the major currently contending hermeneutical camps by relocating the locus of interpretation in the community of interpreters paradigmatically shaped by Royce's concept of the *Beloved Community*. The Beloved Community is based on the general concepts of loyalty and love, and the specific Emersonian concept of *panentheism*, which grounds a holistic view of community within the prehuman orders of nature. This major hermeneutical move is in sympathy with the demand of modernism that rejects pure absolutes and recognizes the Bible as a "time-bound body of insufficiently generic insights." Yet, the skepticism of the Continent, which remains bound by acute subjectivism in reaction to the challenges of modernism, is avoided through a concept of reality that can only be discovered by a community as it works across large stretches of time. In other words, Corrington points a way beyond the impasse of contemporary biblical interpretation in America by establishing that the issues that divide us are fundamentally Continental in origin, and that so-called liberals and conservatives on this side of the Atlantic have far more in common than they think—an insight that has far-reaching implications for American biblical hermeneutics. It is one of the fundamental intentions of the series to lay bare a grammar of discourse that will enable the various biblical interpretive camps to dialogue with one another, thereby releasing the Bible to play a more vital role in the shaping of cultural life and aspirations.

Within the context of the general statements made above, a number of specific issues are raised in Corrington's work that fall directly under the purview of this series. Among these are the following.

1. Corrington argues for a "re-grounding" of the interpretive process in terms of a *horizontal hermeneutics* that is grounded in the dominant cultural ethos of pluralism and democracy. He offers a penetrating discussion of the traits of a fully democratic interpretive community. In addition, he speaks of the communal interpretive horizon as a "midworld" between the individual and the world (including the world of the text). I believe that the recognition of such a midworld at play in our reading of the Bible offers great promise in getting our often-rancorous religious debates away from dead center. In this connection, he makes the important point that all interpretation is *interpretation for another*, an approach that sets the stage for the public reading of the Bible that this series encourages.

2. Corrington does not fall victim to a hermeneutical approach that takes the Bible presuppositionally as an authoritative text. This is important for American biblical hermeneutics, granted the desirability of taking the pluralistic American environment as an operative theological cate-

gory. There is little doubt that the Bible has traditionally played a key role in the formation of the American experience, yet it is fallacious to assume that it *must* continue to do so. In the "brave new world" dominated by science and technology, the Bible must win its own way in the rhetorical terms and categories laid out by the culture. Corrington, building especially upon Royce, crafts a reading of the Bible that is "canonical" in the sense that it reflects the ideals of loyalty and love within the early Christian community that exist in a paradigmatic way for the society as a whole. In this view, canonicity is not something to be authoritatively imposed upon others by the individual believer, or established by ecclesiastical fiat: it is an issue to be investigated within a public context by believers in dialogue with historians, scientists, and philosophers who may or may not share their presuppositions of faith. Such an approach grounds American biblical hermeneutics in the public domain, the only proper avenue open to it in a democratic community.

3. Building upon the thought of Royce, Corrington gives great emphasis in theological discourse to the *Spirit*. Clearly, this is a neglected component of traditional European theological discourse, but one that strikes a strong cord among a significant number of American intellectuals. The intention here is to overcome the logo-centrism of the Continent—including a sympathetic discussion of Emerson's effort to eliminate a closed theological system based on Protestant Biblio-centrism. In some profound sense, the American experience tends to dislodge the absolute claims of Continental thinkers concerning language, and to invite the revelatory powers of Spirit and nature—conceived as the outer form of Spirit—to take its place. Clearly the scientific and naturalistic metaphors utilized in conceiving the "American experiment" carry the corollary of an extremely high regard for nature and, by extension, the Spirit. Such a large amount of investigation remains with regard to both categories within the parameters of the Studies in American Biblical Hermeneutics project. Corrington's work is essential in establishing the philosophical categories to be explored.

4. By definition, American biblical hermeneutics celebrates the priority of the particular over the universal. Corrington provides a strong discussion regarding this point. Following Royce, he notes that *universals can only manifest themselves in particulars and that we do not have access to a special "realm" of genera.* Here he makes reference to the incompleteness of the Bible and, following Royce, the priority of locality/provincialism over universalism. This, in turn, provides a marvelous theoretical foundation for the goal of the series, which is to uncover universal realities that run through the "provinces" rather than to cover up such realities in the name of universalism. In our context, the American experience itself represents such a "province."

Taking all these points into consideration, it is clear that this book communicates the fundamental orientation of the Studies in American

Biblical Hermeneutics series to the interested nonspecialist in biblical studies as well as to the specialist. In that sense, it reaches the public audience for which this series is intended. Just as important, it is also generally programmatic for future work in this area. No better way exists to conclude these opening remarks, perhaps, than with the following quotation from Royce noted by Corrington. This statement could well stand as the hallmark of the entire Studies in American Biblical Hermeneutics series and the challenge that it issues for all of us who labor with the Bible in this milieu:

> My thesis is that, in the present state of the world's civilization, and of the life of our own country, the time has come to emphasize, with a new meaning and intensity, the positive value, the absolute necessity for our own welfare, of a wholesome provincialism, as a saving power to which the world in the near future will need more and more to appeal.[1]

It seems to me that these words are even more true today than they were at the time in which they were written. The tragic flaw of the democratic fruit that has ripened on this continent is a kind of universalism established on the grounds of a vague equality of all religious and philosophical positions. Only a provincialism that forces us to *differentiate* from the *beginning* of our theoretical considerations holds the promise of overcoming this false universalism that otherwise will finally prove to repress the human spirit rather than liberate it.

> *Charles Mabee*
> Marshall University
> 21 September 1987

---

[1]Josiah Royce, *Basic Writings*, ed. John J. McDermott, 2 vols. (Chicago: University of Chicago Press, 1969) 2:1069.

• A U T H O R ' S   P R E F A C E •

The discipline of hermeneutics emerged out of the effort to generalize the tacit principles of biblical exegesis. The subsequent historical development of interpretation theory was responsible for moving hermeneutics away from its inaugural text toward a generic account of meaning per se. Recent work in hermeneutic theory has tended to focus on developments on the Continent. A great deal of attention has been paid to such thinkers as Schleiermacher, Dilthey, Heidegger, Gadamer, Ricoeur, and Derrida. It is assumed that hermeneutic theory is primarily a European achievement and that other philosophical traditions have had little to say concerning the problem of interpretation. The most glaring omission in these historical treatments is that of the American tradition.

In this book I show how such classical American thinkers as Peirce and Royce laid the foundations for a hermeneutics of greater power and scope than that which has evolved in Europe. The problem of the status of nature is raised within the historical context of Emerson's transcendentalism. His decentralizing of the biblical texts in order to establish the priority of nature as the ultimate text represents one of the most important chapters in the history of hermeneutics. Within contemporary American thought, the metaphysics of Justus Buchler is shown to provide the most adequate categorial framework for understanding such persistent hermeneutic problems as the nature of horizons and the structure of the "objects" of hermeneutic query. Buchler's systematic metaphysics represents a fundamental transformation of the very enterprise of philosophy and promises to bear great fruit in the future.

The historical foundations of American hermeneutics, with roots deep within the pragmatic tradition, suggest a number of key conceptual shifts that are moving thought toward what I have called a horizonal hermeneutics. Such a hermeneutics emerges out of dialogue with the thinkers dealt with in this book. Within such hermeneutics four specific areas of reflection find their convergence.

The first area is the development of a theory of community that does justice to the full richness of the interpretive process. Following Royce, I call such a community the community of interpretation. Peirce and Royce each argued that any given interpretation will become validated only insofar as it is manipulated by a given community of interpreters who converge on a common body of signs. Outside such a community, hermeneutics remains tied to the primacy of the isolated subject. The future of hermeneutic theory depends to large extent on its ability to develop and sustain a theory of community that provides the framework within which signs and their interpretations unfold.

The second theme is the utilization of semiotic theory within the context of the community of interpretation. In recent years, semiotics has become an important discipline in its own right. Since much of contemporary sign theory derives its inspiration from the writings of Peirce, it is appropriate that semiotics becomes redefined within the purview of an American hermeneutics. The community has as its object the innumerable sign series that form its interpretive wealth. Semiotics can thus be seen as the dimension of hermeneutics that deals with the intentional objects of interpretation.

The third topic is the rarely undertaken systematic and generic account of the fundamental traits of the world. Continental hermeneutics has self-consciously attacked metaphysics in its efforts to free itself from what it considers to be alien and arbitrary categorial commitments. It should be noted that the American tradition has little sympathy with such attacks on the need for systematic reflection. The ordinal metaphysics of Buchler emerged out of a sustained dialogue with Peirce and Royce and represents the most judicious conceptual framework within which hermeneutic theory can be regrounded. A hermeneutics without a metaphysical horizon is bereft of scope and power.

The fourth area of reflection is the reaffirmation of the supremacy of nature in any theory of interpretation. Contemporary analyses of hermeneutics have drastically overemphasized the manipulative dimension of the human process, which has resulted in a radical perspectivism that sees nature as little more than the blank screen upon which we may exert our projective prowess. Once nature is thus reduced to a secondary status, the supremacy of human textuality takes over. The metaphysical ineptness of this devaluation of nature is evident in the pantextualism that sees everything, whether a person or an event, as a text for which there are no stable or reliable interpretations. The only measure for interpretation is that of the marginal subject and its constituting acts. Such a stress on human constituting acts exemplifies an extreme alienation from the originating impulses that come from a nature ripe with meaning. Nature itself is a hermeneutic process and thus needs to be redefined within the context of a horizonal hermeneutics.

All of these concerns combine to reinforce the view that persons are embedded in a Spirit-filled nature that supports and guides the interpretive process. The specific status of the Judeo-Christian Bible becomes redefined within this understanding of an American hermeneutics. Both Royce and Emerson explicitly grappled with the biblical witness in order to incorporate some key dimensions of it within their respective philosophical horizons. For Royce, Paul emerges as the first hermeneute within the primitive church and as the thinker who both attained and articulated the community of interpretation. For Emerson, Jesus becomes the prototype of the poet who finds a natural grace within the vast orders of a nature explosive with the presence of Spirit. Roycean idealism and Emersonian transcendentalism radically alter our understanding of the meaning and role of the Bible within American culture. In the hermeneutic tradition that emerged from their reflection, the Bible was not so much cast aside as redefined from a different axis of vision. On the positive side, the insights of sacred Scripture were shown to be part and parcel of communal and natural traits that carried their own forms of revelation and grace. On the negative side, the Bible was reduced to the status of a time-bound body of insufficiently generic insights. Hermeneutic theory, emergent out of biblical exegesis, turned back to its origin and relocated the text that gave it birth. Whether the Bible has been well served in this historical inversion is a question for the future.

Among the many people who have helped me with this book, I especially thank Charles Courtney and Frank Oppenheim for helping me clarify my understanding of Royce. I owe my colleague Carl Hausman and my graduate student Felicia Kruse a special debt of gratitude for their always insightful observations on Peirce. They have been especially helpful in showing me some of the intricacies of Peirce's early semiotic. Without the constant encouragement and help of the series editor, Charles Mabee, this book might not have been completed. In addition, I wish to thank my wife, Gail, whose insights into early Christianity and the biblical milieu far transcend mine. Finally, I would like to acknowledge the editors of the *Transactions of the C. S. Peirce Society* for allowing me to reprint substantial portions of my article "A Comparison of Royce's Key Idea of the Community of Interpretation with the Hermeneutics of Gadamer and Heidegger," 20:3 (Summer 1984).

Robert S. Corrington
The Pennsylvania State University
June 1986

THE ORIGINS
OF AMERICAN HERMENEUTICS:
C. S. PEIRCE
AND JOSIAH ROYCE

A self-conscious American hermeneutics can be said to have emerged with the writings of Charles Sanders Peirce (1839-1914) and Josiah Royce (1855-1916). Peirce, trained at Harvard and always a peripheral figure to the academic philosophical establishment, developed a comprehensive metaphysics to which his semiotics and its internal logic was integral. Royce, trained at Johns Hopkins and in Germany, remained at the center of the justly famous Harvard philosophy department during the so-called golden age of American philosophy. Along with William James, George Santayana, and George Palmer, he helped to produce one of the most prominent philosophy departments in the New World. During his long and rich career, Royce developed an absolute idealism that committed him to struggle in order to show the relationship between the realm of the finite and the internal life of the Absolute. In his later years Royce became increasingly influenced by his reading of Peirce's essays and moved toward a more pluralistic understanding of the role of the Absolute in the human community. Peirce's sign theory produced something akin to a conversion experience for the mature Royce. Royce's last major book, *The Problem of Christianity*, published in 1913, presented his mature theory of interpretation and brought Peirce's then-neglected essays into a new prominence.

Royce did not have access to Peirce's unpublished manuscripts until 1915, when they came to Harvard for permanent storage and cataloging. Instead, he relied on the published papers and on Peirce's lectures at Harvard in 1898. Royce specifically mentioned the five articles: "On a New List of Categories" (1867), "Questions concerning Certain Faculties Claimed for Man" (1868-1869), "Some Consequences of Four Incapacities" (1868-1869), "Grounds of the Validity of the Laws of Logic: Further Consequences of Four Incapacities" (1868-1869), and "Sign" (1901).[1]

These articles helped Royce toward his mature vision, in which a rich theory of signs reinforces his epistemology and gives it greater power for the general hermeneutic framework. Peirce's semiotics gave him the tools for developing a hermeneutics and for showing its relation to the community of interpreters. Initially we can define semiotics as the systematic study of those items in experience known as signs. A tendency among semioticians is to define all complexes as signs and to see semiotics as the organon of metaphysics. Peirce was ambivalent on this point but usually restricted the realm of signs to the realm of thought. That is, he argued that all thought must exist in signs, but that which lies outside of thought need not be a sign. Royce himself came close to defining reality as a sign system.[2]

Before I can detail Royce's utilization of Peirce's semiotics, it will be necessary to summarize Peirce's general philosophical position. Our focus will be on elements that have a bearing on the emergence of a hermeneutic perspective.

Peirce is most noted for his creation of the pragmatic movement. The origin of the term *pragmatism* and the creation of the general ideas associated with it can be traced to the Metaphysical Club of the 1870s. Chief among its regular members were Peirce, William James, Justice Holmes, Nicholas St. John Green, John Fiske, and Chauncey Wright. Among the topics discussed were the implications of Darwin's general understanding of evolution, the nature of mind, the nature of belief, the structure of scientific inquiry, and the philosophy of Kant. Pragmatism emerged as a philosophical perspective attuned to evolutionary theory and the critical turn of Kant, which places priority on the constituting power of consciousness.

For Peirce, all ideas were, in essence, plans of action. They could not be seen in atemporal or impractical terms. To frame an idea is to imagine what would follow if the idea were acted on. Science itself is not a mere body of true propositions but functions as a set of leading ideas that contain predictive power. If a given prediction is correct, then it follows that the idea proposed is a proper working hypothesis. The future verification of any idea gives it warrant in the present. Yet Peirce was not committed to a rigid understanding of the formation of these concepts. He insisted that these leading ideas could emerge out of creative and free association.

---

[1] Josiah Royce, *The Problem of Christianity,* ed. John E. Smith (Chicago: University of Chicago Press, 1968) 275-76.

[2] It is not clear just how far Peirce wished to extend the notion of mentality. On one reading, he moved in the direction of panpsychism with his doctrine that matter was effete mind. From this view it would follow that all complexes are to some degree mental. On another reading, he found sign activity in the orders of nature but limited mentality to interpreters.

His technical term for this larger species of ideation is *abduction*. In abduction, as opposed to deduction and induction, ideas can leap beyond the current data and attempt to reach greater generic spread. The process of abduction is related to the process of forming general hypotheses and proceeds beyond simple inductions, which use samples in order to make generalizations from particular instances. Pragmatism takes deduction, induction, and abduction to work together to deepen our grasp of nature and its traits. Science progresses by making use of each method as called for by the matter under investigation.

Integral to Peirce's pragmatism is the notion that our leading ideas are fallible; that is, we cannot have apodictic certainty about any general or particular claims. This position is of a piece with Peirce's rejection of foundationalism in several of its forms. Epistemological foundationalism claims that knowledge originates in or arrives at an indubitable "given" that functions to validate all truth claims. Metaphysical foundationalism claims that one class or genus will prevail as the ultimate reality from which all others are derived. In the philosophy of mind, foundationalism appears as the belief in a final substantive self that can be isolated by some sort of simple intuition. Pragmatism rejects all three forms of foundationalism because they advance claims that violate the fallibilism of general abduction. Furthermore, fallibilism is a part of every interpretive process and cannot be overcome by any form of methodic reflection. There are no "pure" givens, and there is no such thing as an intuited soul-substance. All leading ideas must be tested against changing experience, and the verdict must often be delayed.

While ideas are fallible and emerge through tentative probings, they also form themselves into habitual patterns. Like William James, Peirce was impressed with the power of habit to mold and govern the process of ideation. Underlying this belief in the habitual structure of ideas is his metaphysical belief that nature itself evolves into certain patterns that can best be described as habits. The so-called laws of nature are the habits that prevail at a given cosmic epoch. These habits are subject to change across long stretches of time and can reform themselves in new and novel patterns. The centrality of the concept of habit in both his epistemology and cosmology provides a metaphysical justification for both fallibilism and open-endedness.

Peirce's pragmatism is thus future directed and open to novelty. Underlying this framework is the strong belief that reality cannot be adequately known by an individual. Since knowledge is fallible and since nature itself is subject to novel variation (the doctrine of "tychism"), the individual must rely on others for some form of reliable knowledge. No individual could hope to make all of the necessary interpretive steps that would ensure that both habit and novelty were fully grasped. For Peirce, the community of science and its investigators is the most adequate horizon for the quest for truth. Such a community can combine many insights and talents in order to arrive at some consensus. The community of science became normative for Peirce because of its self-corrective nature. That is, all knowledge claims became subject to further analysis and evaluation. The scientific community welcomes the counterexample that would force it to rethink the abductive inferences of its general theories. Peirce insisted that the scientific method, and its use as integral to a community of science, was preferable to the methods of authority, tenacity, or a priori reasoning.

Peirce was not content with only showing how knowledge functions; he saw his role as that of the philosopher in search of first principles. Rather than reduce reality to one ultimate principle, Peirce proposed three fundamental, nonreducible categories to which all more complex categories could be reduced. He thus divided reality into the three categories of "firstness," "secondness," and "thirdness." Firstness can be described as the category of bare immediacy. That is, it deals with pure, undiscriminated presence. Epistemologically, firstness is an immediate and vivid but indescribable experience. Metaphysically, firstness is possibility that could become qualities that are general, such as redness or pain. In either case, firstness is characterized as that which is vivid, immediate, unorganized, unreflected, and uncognized; yet general traits (qualities) can emerge in metaphysical firstness.

Secondness, by contrast, is characterized by its resistance to our intentions or expectations. Epistemologically, secondness is experienced as a shock to habitual patterns of awareness. It is particular and disruptive. Metaphysically, secondness is characterized as the nonego, or what is other. That is, it cannot be associated with the self, since it actively contradicts the volitions of the self.

Thirdness depends upon both firstness and secondness and functions as their mediation. Thirdness is conceptual and conscious. It is the realm of general, repeatable experiences and, in general, is cognitive. All uniformities, in knowledge or reality, are modes of thirdness insofar as they are general. Human action is governed by the thirdness that is cognitively present. Without thirds we would be left with the confusing and uncognizable world of immediacy and resistance.

All three categories function to show how knowledge and reality are inseparable. Pragmatism is in search of thirdness, as thirdness guarantees that general ideas have been found that govern and order experience. The resistance provided by secondness directs us in a variety of ways by eliminating false paths. Any time a theory oversteps its bounds, reality will resist its claims by behaving in ways not accounted for. This resistance persists until the theory becomes attuned to the reality under investigation. Firstness gives knowledge its initial immediacy and vividness. A qualitative whole supports thought as it attempts to penetrate into the trait constitution of a complex. All three categories function together to enrich and guide the leading ideas of pragmatic inquiry. Peirce was aware that no epistemology could function without these proper metaphysical underpinnings. His three categories gave him the structures for showing how knowledge functions.

The three categories were given concrete content by Peirce's elaborate theory of signs. Thought cannot function without signs. Human understanding thus consists of the assimilation and manipulation of signs. Peirce lavished great care on the various distinctions between types of signs. A basic distinction, however, identifies three: icon, index, and symbol. While his sign theory includes many other distinctions, this triad pertains to the way signs relate to objects.

A sign refers to an object in a certain way and makes an interpretation of that object available to an interpreter. Each sign links up with other signs to form a sign series with neither beginning nor end. As it does so, it functions as an icon, as an index, or as a symbol (or as some combination of the three). As an icon, a sign signifies by virtue of its resemblance to that to which it refers. For example, a map is an iconic sign of a terrain because its shapes and lines are roughly isomorphic with the landscape. Photographs and paintings are iconic signs because of their pictorial immediacy. As an index, a sign points to something because of an existential relation the object has with the sign. Some existential relations may be causal and some may be spatio-temporal. For example, a stop sign directs driving behavior without physically representing the actual situation. Physical symptoms and natural events can function indexically. Thus a certain cloud formation can be an index of impending rain. While an indexical sign refers to a particular, a symbolic sign refers to a general class or group of things. A symbol, unlike an icon, need not have a form in common with its object. Language, for example, functions symbolically, as do images and tones. Symbols are grounded in general laws or habits of nature and are necessary for the stabilization and advancement of knowledge.

Icons, indexes, and symbols are never found in their pure forms except on a theoretical level. Peirce refers to this process of abstraction from concrete cases as "prescinding." That is, we turn attention away from a given functioning sign in order to isolate its separate moments or aspects. Furthermore, any given sign may function in all three modes. A sign may emphasize one mode and exhibit the others in what Peirce calls a "degenerate" form. The notion of a degenerate sign form or category is not to be understood normatively. In our present context, the term *degenerate* simply means that one or two forms are less prevalent than the remainder. For example, an actor's gesture on a stage can function in each of the three sign modes. The sweep of the arm outward can function iconically to reinforce the overall qualitative sense of a scene fraught with tension. The same gesture can function indexically to give another actor the cue to walk offstage. Finally, the movement of the arm can also convey the sense that the character referred to by the gesture belongs to a class of persons who symbolize evil. A stage director might be very interested in the gesture as an icon and as an index, while a literary critic might be more concerned with its symbolic value for the playwright or the audience. In either case, one or more dimensions of the sign are selected for particular attention. The other dimensions are present in a weaker form.

Signs of all three forms are necessary for communication and community. Philosophy focuses on the symbolic function of signs in order to grasp the conceptual dimension of a given sign or sign series. This emphasis entails the view that philosophy is concerned with thirdness, that is, with the general laws and habits of persons and the world. Such general categories are deposited in symbols.

Peirce's semiotics functions to flesh out his general metaphysical categories of firstness, secondness, and thirdness. Icons present the immediacy of firstness. Indexical signs exhibit the physical resistance of secondness. Symbols show general laws and habits, the realm of thirdness. Here we can see that Peirce insisted that semiotics is the logic of metaphysics.

Since anything intelligible is a sign, it follows that our general understanding of the basic traits of the world must be rendered into semiotic terms. Semiotic is the organon of metaphysics insofar as it articulates the rules of meaning and interpretation. Once the general logic of signs is developed, it becomes possible to find a reliable framework for the kind of generic analysis that prevails most effectively in metaphysics.

Finally, Peirce developed a cosmology that attempted to account for the development of the general categories. In addition to the notion *tychism* (chance) are Peirce's categories *synechism* and *agapism*. Peirce saw all of reality as a continuum. All so-called individuals blend together into series or units that can only artificially be divided. Time, for example, appears to be constituted by discrete units that can be divided off from each other. A more careful examination of the movement of time, however, reveals that there are no discrete instants that can be isolated and defined. Rather, the "moments" of time are infinitesimals that blend together to form a series with neither beginning nor end. This Bergson-like view applies to all reality. Whatever is, is part of a continuum. Peirce called this general principle of inner connectedness synechism. It serves to exhibit the tendency of nature and thought toward unity and wholeness. Many continua prevail in nature, even if they do not all function in the same way.

Agapism, the third general principle of Peirce's cosmology, affirms that there is a principle of evolutionary love that operates in the universe as a whole. Agape lets growth develop freely without a predetermined goal, but at the same time growth is toward a more perfect state of harmony. While the principle of synechism refers to the continua in nature, the principle of agapism refers to the spontaneity and movement of nature. Our current cosmic epoch is characterized by imperfection and incompletion and must be surpassed in the future by a cosmos more attuned to God's divine love and harmony. The general habits (thirds) of nature are moving toward an ideal convergence in which, in an infinite future, the disharmony of secondness would be gathered in a perfected state.[3]

Agapism is the most controversial of Peirce's three cosmic principles. Many arguments have been advanced supporting something akin to tychism and synechism, but few thinkers would defend the view that the cosmos is evolving toward universal love. Royce came to affirm all three principles in a modified form. His belief in tychism can be seen in his hermeneutics, where he advocates an open-ended view of sign translation and comparison. Creative chance is an essential part of this process. His belief in synechism can be seen in his sign theory, where he establishes that signs must link together to form a series that cannot admit of diremption, or a fundamental discontinuity. His belief in agapism can be seen in his affirmation of the "Beloved Community," which will emerge from the natural and living communities of interpretation. The Beloved Community stands as both the inner telos and the outer lure for the hermeneutic communities of our everyday standpoint.

In examining the specific ways in which Royce was influenced by Peirce, we must focus on the above-mentioned essays written by Peirce in the 1860s. In these papers, Peirce is struggling to find a proper language for his understanding of sign function and the theory of the self that such a semiotic entails. General problems of methodology are central to his argument for a new conception of interpretation and become the basis for Royce's own attempts to develop a general hermeneutics.

The first essay, "On a New List of Categories," was published in 1867 and represents Peirce's attempt to show how the manifold of experience is brought into order through signs. In it he gives some indication of the nature of objects and of our knowledge of them. Objects are general in some degree and exist for us, the interpreters, as signs. "The objects of the understanding, considered as representations, are symbols, that is, signs which are at least potentially general. But the rules of logic hold good of any symbols, of those which are written or spoken as well as those which are thought."[4] Any object of the understanding must have some general predicate that itself is embodied in the sign. Logic is concerned with the relation between general predicates. Universals are held to be real, not nominal, and to inhere in particulars. Objects without these uni-

---

[3]For an evocative analysis of Peirce's understanding of agapism, see Carl R. Hausman, "Eros and Agape in Creative Evolution: A Peircean Insight," *Process Studies* 4:1 (Spring 1974): 11-25.

[4]Charles S. Peirce, *The Collected Papers*, vols. 1-6, ed. C. Hartshorne and P. Weiss (Cambridge MA: Harvard University Press, 1931-1935) 1.559. Subsequent citations are noted in the text and refer to this edition.

versal traits are not cognizable. All universals are expressed in signs, which means that all thought of these universals must be in signs.

To think or to experience is to use signs. This use can occur either in a controlled manner, as in induction, or in a manner of imaginative association, in what Peirce calls "interpretive musement." This musement allows signs to unfold in creative and novel patterns. Chance, or tychism, is manifest in this open-ended method. The manipulation of signs in this open way is part of the general abductive process that frames hypotheses that go beyond the data at any given time.

Peirce lays the foundation for his mature view of the nature of signs by speaking of three elements or functions within a given sign. The first is its *denotation*, which is its reference to an object. The second is its *connotation*, which is its reference to a ground of meaning—a ground larger than its denotation. The third element or function is the *information conveyed* by the sign to an interpreter. Peirce states,

> There is, first, the direct reference of a symbol to its objects, or to its denotation; second, the reference of the symbol to its ground, through its object, that is, its reference to the common characters of its objects, or its connotation; and third, its reference to its interpretants through its object, that is, its reference to all the synthetic propositions in which its objects in common are subject or predicate, and this I term the information it embodies. (1.559)

The third element consists in the sum of propositions referring to both the subject and the predicate. Thus both thirdness, as the web of the predicates, and the subject are presented in this third function of signs. The object is brought into unity by the sign, which establishes the relation between the background (manifold) and the denoted particular.

For example, a text can be seen as a complex sign or as a sign series. Insofar as it conveys information, say, about a historical epoch, its signs function on the third level, in which the reader, as interpreter, is brought into relation to the web of meanings. Insofar as the same text functions as a unity and exhibits some common traits in its depiction of history, it functions on the second level. Finally, insofar as the text refers to actual events and persons in the order of history, it functions on the first level. Any sign will have all three elements, although one or two may be more central to a given sign.

The sign unifies the object with its traits and with the resulting interpretation (information). Furthermore, signs preserve the relations that obtain between subjects and predicates. This keeps the whole object in view and forces further signs to conform to the semiotic structures exhibited in the object. Subject, predicate, denotation, and background are all preserved in the sign function. Signs also link together with other signs to create and sustain a picture of reality.

Peirce did not rest content with fixing the threefold nature of signs. Rather, he probed into the nature of mind and knowledge in an effort to establish the actual role of signs in the generation of scientific and everyday knowledge. His most important statement of these larger, very early semiotic concerns is in his 1868 essay "Questions concerning Certain Faculties Claimed for Man." In this essay he attempts to demolish certain Cartesian claims made about the way knowledge functions within ongoing mental life. Four specific beliefs are attacked: the belief in introspection, the belief in pure intuition, the belief that we can think without signs, and the belief that there is something noncognizable, that is, an unknown thing-in-itself. All of these Cartesian views were also criticized by Royce.

As part of his general pragmatic or pragmaticist program, Peirce rejects foundationalism, or the belief that philosophy has primitive, self-evident first principles. We cannot, simply by reflection or intuition, immediately grasp the first principles of reality. Furthermore, it is impossible to have an intuitive or introspective knowledge of our own minds. There can be no absolute beginning point for our internal or external cognitions. Any experience or thought is thus determined by previous experiences or thoughts, which form a series. In this semiotic continuum there is no first sign. We plunge into the middle of a series and must obey the semiotic structures already attained.

Not only does thought exist in a continuum, but it cannot exist unless embodied in signs. In Peirce's words,

> If we seek the light of external facts, the only cases of thought which we can find are thoughts in signs. Plainly, no other thought can be evidenced by external facts. But we have seen that only by external facts can thought be known at all. The only thought, then, which can possibly be cognized is thought in signs. But thought which cannot be cognized does not exist. All thought, therefore, must necessarily be in signs. (5.251)

Royce makes this insight central to the second half of *The Problem of Christianity*, where its implications are carefully developed for hermeneutics. From Peirce's perspective this stress on the necessity for signs solves epistemological problems about the nature of absolute simples, or simple sense-data. We can no longer rely on the simples of Locke, which attempt to jump out of the living continuum of thought and experience. We may select a given sign for analysis, but this step is only a methodic and momentary intrusion into the semiotic continuum. All signs refer to at least one other sign and exist within a sign matrix. That is, signs form living communities.

If every thought is a sign and every sign must refer to at least one other sign, it follows that thoughts determine other thoughts and that no thought is isolated. Peirce puts the case as follows:

> From the proposition that every thought is a sign, it follows that every thought must address itself to some other, must determine some other, since that is the essence of a sign. This, after all, is but another form of the

> familiar axiom that in intuition, i.e., in the immediate present, there is no thought, or that all which is reflected upon has past. . . . To say, therefore, that thought cannot happen in an instant, but requires a time, is but another way of saying that every thought must be interpreted in another, or that all thought is in signs. (5.253)

To think in signs is to think across a temporal continuum. A pure atemporal experience is an impossibility. Furthermore, as noted above, all thought is determined by previous thoughts. No given cognition could remove itself from the pressure of the semiotic series. Thought is relational and serial. For Peirce, as for Royce, atomism is an impossible doctrine. No sign is free from the felt pressure of the past signs that form its specific series.

Given the above statements it is no surprise that Peirce rejects the notion of a first cognition. We always find ourselves in the middle of a semiotic continuum. Yet Peirce does allow for lines of convergence within this continuum. These semiotic lines are directed toward the future and point to an ideal fulfillment. This fulfillment or completion can come only from the community that has the necessary internal constitution for following the series across time. Once again, the hermeneutic problem gets translated into the problem of the community and the signs at its disposal. For Peirce, the ideal community is that of science, which welcomes counterexamples to its abductive generalizations. Royce takes this Peircean model and stretches it into the more generic model of the community of interpretation. In either model, signs cannot be fully grasped outside of a living community. All hermeneutic acts are communal.

Later in 1868, Peirce published "Some Consequences of Four Incapacities," in which he expands upon his notion of community.

> We individually cannot reasonably hope to attain the ultimate philosophy which we pursue; we can only seek it, therefore, for the community of philosophers. Hence if disciplined and candid minds carefully examine a theory and refuse to accept it, this ought to create doubts in the mind of the author of the theory himself. (5.265)

This follows from Peirce's rejection of pure intuition and the alleged self-evidence of first principles. For if we must enter the sign series at the middle, it follows that at least part of that series was forged by someone or something—some thought—other than myself. Simply to perceive an object is to use signs that have been developed by others. To recognize the color blue, for example, is to know just how to use the color manifold in specific ways. The initial "slice" of this discrimination comes to us from the past of the community and its historical discrimination. Furthermore, given that we cannot have absolute simples, it follows that signs must exhibit relations that go beyond the power of a given interpreter. Could one person hope to grasp the semiotic structure of a historically important event? This feat would require the consort of many, if not an infinite number of, interpreters.

Truth itself—that is, the agreement of signs with reality—cannot be won by one interpreter. Peirce is here stressing what one might call a nonheroic conception of the role of the individual philosopher. To do philosophy is to compare one's general symbols with those of other thinkers. Only through such endless comparisons can we expect to arrive at the proper list of categories for understanding the general contour of reality. This completion remains in the future and in the conditional. Peirce, unlike Kant, is concerned with what would be the case in the future, given certain signs and interpretations in the present. Kant remains tied to the present and the static application of the table of judgments to the manifold of sense intuition. When Peirce shifts the truth problem to one involving conditional statements in a ideal future, he shows the intimate relation between the categories and an ongoing process of inquiry. Kant's hidden thing-in-itself becomes a would-be in the future. This counterfactual conditional is an ideal limit because it functions as the hoped-for actuality.

Since all knowledge is in and through signs, it follows that knowledge of the self occurs through signs. We cannot posit a self-substance that remains the same throughout various transformations. Rather, the self must be seen as a sign series. According to Peirce,

> When we think, then, we ourselves, as we are at that moment, appear as a sign. Now a sign has, as such, three references: first, it is a sign to some thought which interprets it; second, it is a sign for some object to which in that thought it is equivalent; third, it is a sign, in some respect or quality, which brings it into connection with its object. (5.283)

We are signs to ourselves, and signs themselves function in the threefold manner discussed above. A sign refers to an object (denotation) in some way (connotation) and to some thought (interpretant). Thus when we look into ourselves we must follow this general threefold pattern. We see our self in some respect, and our seeing produces an interpretant or thought about the self. This process is complicated by being temporal. We are always in the dilemma of finding the relation between past, present, and possible future selves. The problem is compounded because each sign (self-interpretation) is part of a continuum that has no absolute beginning or end. The result is that we have more than one self.

The process of self-understanding is endless. Only death can stop the process. Murray Murphey puts this conclusion quite succinctly.

> Peirce's analysis of signs leads to a further conclusion. If every sign must have an interpretant, and the interpretant is itself a sign, then the series of signs not only has no beginning—it also has no end. This conclusion, also, Peirce fully endorsed. The infinite series of signs may be interrupted by

death or other factors, but of itself the sign process goes on forever. Thus thinking is an endless process of sign interpretation.[5]

The sign series that forms my self thus has no natural terminus other than death, a feature common to all sign series, both internal and external. No object can ever be fully interpreted, in that the signs depicting it must be subject to reinterpretation within the flow of time and the given sign series. Only in a ideal future will the sign series reach full convergence and total transparency.

But signs do not disappear into the object to be represented. Signs have properties that are not to be found in the referent. This is so even with iconic signs, which otherwise share traits with their referent. Peirce calls the independence of the sign, taken in itself, its *material quality* and analyzes it as follows:

> Since a sign is not identical with the thing signified, but differs from the latter in some respects, it must plainly have some characters which belong to it in itself, and have nothing to do with its representative function. These I call the material qualities of the sign. As examples of such qualities, take in the word *man*, its consisting of three letters—in a picture, its being flat and without relief. In the second place, a sign must be capable of being connected (not in the reason but really) with another sign of the same object, or with the object itself. Thus words would be of no value at all unless they could be connected into sentences by means of a real copula which joins signs of the same thing. (5.287)

This analysis applies to signs in all three modes: iconic, indexical, and symbolic. A sign thus has this dual quality. On the one hand, it must remain distinct from its referent, such as the English letters m, a, and n in conjunction and the real genus of beings denoted by the term. On the other hand, the word *man* must have some meaningful connection with such words or phrases as "rational animal" and "featherless biped." Yet it is not clear from this example just how the word *man* connects to the real genus, given that the iconic function is degenerate. The connection has to be conventional rather than natural and is thus more subject to change or alteration.

This semiotic structure has implications for more traditional analyses of the relation of thought and experience. Peirce, like Royce, had little faith in orthodox British empiricism, with its insistence upon simple ideas of impression. Empiricism fails to recognize the ubiquity of signs and the impossibility of finding any so-called pure simples. Peirce insisted that we have complex sign functions that connect the mind to reality in a variety of ways.

---

[5]Elizabeth Flower and Murray G. Murphey, *A History of Philosophy in America*, 2 vols. (New York: Capricorn Books, 1977) 2:578.

Furthermore, the traditional notion of the association of ideas as developed by Locke and Hume fails to show the true and varied connection among ideas. Peirce subsumes association under inference. "So, then, the association of ideas consists in this, that a judgment occasions another judgment, of which it is the sign. Now this is nothing less nor more than inference. . . . All association is by signs" (5.307, 309). The traditional Humean principles of resemblance, contiguity, and causality can all be dealt with under the semiotic analysis of experience. To find a resemblance between two experiences (impressions) is thus to make an inference from one sign to another that the signs refer to something that has at least one important trait in common with something else. The movement between areas of experience is actually inferential, even if the specific steps of a given inference are hidden to the interpreter. Hence we can conclude that experience, even at its most primitive level, is funded by interpretation and inference.

The tendency of the associated signs is toward some sort of unbounded series. A given sign will thus be determined by both its antecedents and its consequents. Its truth value will never be fully determinable in a given instance. Peirce thus adds the crucial temporal element to the traditional empirical analysis. The ultimate tendency of a given sign series can be determined only by a community of inquiry. The series must be ramified and studied through time. Reality—that which is determined by sign series—can be discovered only by a community as it works across large stretches of time.

> The real, then, is that which, sooner or later, information and reasoning would finally result in, and which is therefore independent of the vagaries of me and you. Thus, the very origin of the conception of reality shows that this conception essentially involves the notion of a COMMUNITY, without definite limits, and capable of a definite increase of knowledge. And so these two series of cognition—the real and the unreal—consist of those which, at a time sufficiently future, the community will always continue to reaffirm; and of those which, under the same conditions, will ever after be denied. (5.311)

This passage is essential to an understanding of the relation between Peirce and Royce. The community now stands as the place where knowledge is won or lost, and the community can work across large stretches of time to ensure that knowledge will indeed be won. We will see the post-1912 Royce using this idea to replace the notion of the Absolute Self as the guarantor of our truth claims. For both thinkers, the community enables us to go beyond private experience and to provide objective criteria for distinguishing between the veridical and the false. Furthermore, the community has no pregiven limits to its articulation and ramification of signs and the various series into which they evolve. The community has the necessary internal structure for dealing with the complexity of signs. The relation between semiotics and the philosophy of community was quite clear to both thinkers. Signs are complex in their denotative and connotative functions. Signs also have a natural tendency to link together into a series. Finally, signs are always signs for someone, namely, an interpreter. The interpreter has the function of interpreting the given sign to another. Thus we can see how signs can be understood only within the complex structures of a community.

To add to this insight we must remind ourselves of what was said about the nature of the self. The self is, in essence, a private community. Since we have no direct introspective evidence of our "rock-bottom" self, we must remain content with a glimpse into the series of signs, qua interpretations, that go into the articulation of the many part-selves within us. As individuals we are the sum total of our signs to ourselves and to others. These signs are rendered into language and become external expressions of our nature.

> For, as the fact that every thought is a sign, taken in conjunction with the fact that life is a train of thought, proves that man is a sign; so, that every thought is an *external* sign, proves that man is an external sign. That is to say, the man and the external sign are identical, in the same sense in which the words *homo* and *man* are identical. Thus my language is the sum total of myself; for the man is the thought. (5.314)

We externalize our signs through language and thus are in a position to discover who we are internally. Yet what we discover is never the simple monistic self of introspection but a sign series rendered in public language. Peirce went beyond the earlier hermeneutic formulation of Schleiermacher by insisting that the expressions of language do not reveal a substantive self-consciousness with one determinate, if evolving, nature. We do not necessarily know the "author better than he knew himself," as it is unclear just what ontological status the self would have. Both Peirce and Royce came to see the self in semiotic terms and thus raised the problem of self-identity to new levels of complexity and interest. Yet, like Schleiermacher, they believed that our external expressions are a fair indication of our internal nature, however complex that nature may be.

In the fourth article mentioned by Royce, we can see a few further implications of the semiotic analysis of experience and knowledge. In the 1868 article "Grounds of the Validity of the Laws of Logic: Further Conences of Four Incapacities," Peirce moves toward a social theory of logic and its applications. The simplicity of the syllogism is rejected in favor of the linkage between signs in a social series. This rethinking of logic carries with it some novel metaphysical insights.

Returning to earlier analyses, Peirce reaffirms his belief that knowledge has no primitive beginning but is part of a continuous process with neither first element nor last.

> It is true, that since some judgment precedes every judgment inferred, either the first premises were not inferred, or there have been no first

premisses. But it does not follow that because there has been no first in a series, therefore that series has had no beginning in time; for the series may be continuous, and may have begun gradually, as was shown in an article in this volume, where this difficulty has already been resolved. (5.327)

We cannot rely upon some noninterpretive intuition of a neutral given. The specific signs under analysis belong, by definition, to a series of inferences that reach back to a point perhaps out of immediate cognitive reach. Yet there is no reason to assume that the chain of inference can be reversed to reveal basic axioms or foundational principles. Whenever we make a judgment we are part of a moving series of signs and judgments. Continuity is a part of any semiotic structure.

From this it does not follow that our inferences have no direction or internal regulation. The basis for any given inference will be found within the semiotic structure and within the communal ramifications that unfold it. Logic can no longer rely upon unquestioned premises but must reflect the social reality within which signs and inferences move. The logical structure is not dyadic but triadic. A simple step-by-step process of deduction is replaced by branching relations. The process is triadic in that each inference refers to both an interpreter and an interpretee. It is never a simple truth function but belongs within a human community of branching relations and inferences. The triadic nature of logical relation is wedded to community. According to Peirce,

> He who recognizes the logical necessity of complete self-identification of one's own interests with those of the community, and its potential existence in man, even if he has it not himself, will perceive that only the inferences of that man who has it are logical, and so views his own inferences as being valid only so far as they are accepted by that man. But so far as he has this belief, he becomes identified with that man. And that ideal perfection of knowledge by which we have seen that reality is constituted must thus belong to a community in which this identification is complete. (5.356)

Knowledge, which itself is based on signs, can be won only when the individual identifies with the life of the community. For Peirce, the ideal model for the perfect community is the community of science. The scientific community is a self-corrective domain of free inquiry into the semiotic structures of objects and events. The community renews itself by placing all inferences under the skeptical eye of the researchers, who are dedicated to the search for counterexamples. The community has the teleological drive toward that ideal future in which scientific knowledge is secure and based on general metaphysical principles such as that of agapism. Peirce wished to generalize from the pragmatically guided scientific community at large, but it was Royce who fulfilled the project of exhibiting the nature of community in the fullest sense as the community of interpretation.

The ontology of the community was developed by both Peirce and Royce. Royce used the semiotics of the 1860s papers but drove beyond

Peirce's notion of community to arrive at a broadly conceived and richly drawn understanding of the horizonal structures of true interpretive communities.

Peirce enabled Royce to make the living human community central to his evolving hermeneutics. The community became the place where interpretations are tested and validated. This shift in emphasis reduced the role of the Absolute Mind as the guarantor of our hermeneutic acts. Yet Royce, as we shall see, added an essential religious dimension to community by his detailed conception of the community of the early Christian church and by his eschatological hope for a universal and Beloved Community.

From Peirce, Royce derived the idea that reality consists of signs and sign relations. Furthermore, and perhaps more important, he realized that hermeneutics requires a semiotic dimension if it is to treat all objects of interpretation adequately. He did not, however, retain the distinction between iconic, indexical, and symbolic signs but focused instead on the social and relational dimensions of sign systems.

Royce become increasingly pluralistic as his thought evolved. Peirce's belief in the endlessness of interpretation and sign articulation undercut the belief in a final atemporal view of truth. This pluralism was reinforced by the temporal analysis of sign interpretation. Royce came to realize that knowledge must evolve across time and must take more forms than monism allows.

Peirce's rejection of the older substance view of the self helped Royce toward the view that the individual is actually a microcosmic community and is constituted by sign series. The hermeneutic problem was enriched by the semiotic theory of the self and enabled Royce to see that the knowledge problem was of greater complexity than his earlier absolutism thought possible. Both the Absolute Self and the finite self were redefined.

Royce gathered these Peircean insights together and grounded them within his own evolving idealism to create a hermeneutic theory of great scope and power. In 1913 he published *The Problem of Christianity,* which represents the essence of his mature view of community and interpretation. The sixteen chapters range over a number of topics directly and indirectly related to hermeneutics. Specifically, Royce presents his understanding of the Christian religion and of the interpretive process as it unfolds within the community. The doctrine of the Absolute is rethought in terms of the universal community of interpretation.

In dealing with the interpretive process, Royce covers a number of issues central to his earlier writing. Chief among these are the nature of loyalty, the structure of the community, human sin, atonement, the psychology of interpretation, and the limitations of pragmatism. In addition he introduces important reflections on the nature of the primitive church and the hermeneutic role of the Apostle Paul. In chapter four, I detail his analysis of the Pauline Epistles as they pertain to the hermeneutic problem of interpreting the sayings of Jesus. In the remaining part of this chapter we consider his articulation of the principles of general hermeneutics, matters he treats in the second half of *The Problem of Christianity*.

Royce starts his analysis by insisting that his description of the Universal Community has its metaphysical basis in the sign of the Logos-Spirit, which will lead participants in that community into a transfigured notion of God. He states,

> Central among these ideas is that of the Universal Community. For us, then, theology, if we are to define theology at all, must depend upon the metaphysical interpretation and foundation of the community. If that ideal of one beloved and united community of all mankind whose religious value we have defended, has a basis, not merely in the transient interests of us mortals, but also in whatever is largest and most lasting in the universe, then indeed the doctrine of the community will prove to be a doctrine about the being and nature and manifestation of God; and our estimate of the relation of the modern mind to the spirit of a Christian creed will be altered and completed accordingly.[6]

The community is the proper manifestation of God in time and history. The Absolute of Royce's earlier period has been concretized as the actual concrete community of the Universal Church. The natural communities that prevail in history are in search of greater and greater expansion in the hopes of attaining a world-uniting power. Each particular community is thus moving toward the Universal Community, which is the kingdom to be attained both at the end of time and at the consummation of human historical evolution.

Royce insists that the Holy Spirit provides the unity and direction for the community. Without the agency of this Spirit the community could not prevail against the corrosive forces of solipsism and aggressive individualism. No mere random collection of individuals will constitute a genuine community. An aggregate of selves functions without a common memory or a common future. For Royce, "A true community is essentially a product of a time-process. A community has a past and will have a future. Its more or less conscious history, real or ideal, is a part of its very essence. A community requires for its existence a history and is greatly aided in its consciousness by memory" (243). Thus a true community has at least some events in the past that are consciously shared by its members. Furthermore, it will have common hopes and aspirations for the future. Without this spread across time the collection of individuals would not have sufficient convergence to form a viable community. A common history or common ancestors are required to have what Royce

---

[6]Royce, *Problem of Christianity*, 232-33. Subsequent citations are noted in the text and refer to this edition.

calls a "community of memory," while some common hopes are required to have a "community of expectation" (248).

The hermeneutic problem is felt acutely at this point, in that the community must now attempt to deal with the proper criteria for interpreting its felt past and projected future. How is the community to know its past? What criteria of discrimination between truth and falsehood are to be applied? Can a community exist without some form of collective idealization of its past?

Royce indicates that the Spirit will serve to ensure given truth claims and to establish their interpretive precision. Yet it is not fully clear how collective myths can be deconstructed or corrected when they fail to convey the proper aspects of the imagined past. Do we have an objective basis for testing the hermeneutic choices of the Spirit? Can we even talk of an extraspiritual validation for hermeneutics? An answer to this cluster of questions begins to emerge when we look at Royce's rethinking of semiotics and communal interpretations.

Royce initiates his reflections on interpretation by reminding us that the word itself is one that should be familiar.

> In defining what constitutes a community I have repeatedly mentioned processes of Interpretation. The word *interpretation* is well known; and students of the humanities have special reasons for using it frequently. When one calls an opinion about the self an interpretation, one is not employing language that is familiar only to philosophers. . . . And the process of interpretation, whatever it is, is intended to meet human needs which are as well known as they are vital. Such needs determine, as we shall see, whatever is humane and articulate in the whole conduct and texture of our lives. (273)

Royce here indicates that interpretation is vital to the success of civilization. It is a general mental process that is as universal as it is inevitable. Yet the reflection on the nature of interpretation in its everydayness brings us into the heart of philosophy and metaphysics.

Not only is interpretation a part of every private perception or thought, it is essential to both the self and its community. Royce relates self-identity to communal identity through his understanding of interpretation.

> A community, as we have seen, depends for its very constitution upon the way in which each of its members interprets himself and his life. For the rest, nobody's self is either a mere datum or an abstract conception. A self is a life whose unity and connectedness depend upon some sort of interpretation of plans, of memories, of hopes, and of deeds. If, then, there are communities, there are many selves who, despite their variety, so interpret their lives that all these lives, taken together, get the type of unity which our last lecture characterized. Were there, then, no interpretations in the world, there would be neither selves nor communities. (274)

To be a self is to be a series of interpretations that are partly derived from the communal structure. This series is temporal and entails three selves:

the past, the present, and the future. The present self interprets past and future selves in terms of its current but changing self-image. The sum to-tal of all such images (signs) constitutes personal identity. Royce care-fully links this process of self-identity to the process of generating a community. Each individual comes to identify with a past shared in com-mon and also to affirm future goals and aspirations. From the struggle for self-identity thus come the above-mentioned "community of memory" and "community of expectation."

At no time can the self or its community rely upon simple sense-data or bare conceptions. Rather, self and social knowledge consist in the ma-nipulation and assimilation of signs and sign series. The act of interpre-tation, which we make automatically as well as, on rarer occasions, consciously, is a third operation that cannot be reduced to either percep-tion or conception.

Royce reiterates Peirce's view that knowledge is triadic rather than dyadic and that the interpretive process is distinct in nature and function from either perception or conception. He states,

> Despite this prevalence of the dual classification of our cognitive process, most of us will readily acknowledge that, in our real life, we human beings are never possessed either of pure perception or of pure conception. In ideal, we can define an intuitive type of knowledge, which should merely see, and which should never think. In an equally ideal fashion, we can imagine the possibility of a pure thought, which should have as its sole real object a realm of universals, and which should ignore all sensible data. But we mortals live the intelligent part of our lives through some sort of more or less imperfect union or synthesis of conception and perception. (278)

The dyadic model of perception/conception does not reflect the actual phenomenological data that insist that we can never find a "pure" thought or a "pure" perception. Royce insists that universals can manifest them-selves only in particulars and that we do not have access to a special realm of genera. The parallels with Hegel's concrete universals should not be overlooked. Interpretations and their symbolic cores present and pre-serve general truths for the community. The Absolute functions as both the Spirit of Interpretation and as the realm of attained and attainable concrete universals.

Knowledge, as interpretation, must be triadic. However, Royce under-stands the triadic function in two ways. The first triad links perception and conception into an interpretation. The second triad links the person, object, or event interpreted to the person for whom the interpretation is under-taken. That is, an interpreter interprets something or someone for the in-terpretee. This second form of the triadic relation is in part asymmetrical in that the process of interpretation cannot be reversed. It has a given temporal and interpretive direction and a built-in compulsion. Royce describes this second type of triadic function as follows:

> Thus an interpretation is a relation which not only involves three terms, but brings them into a determinate order. One of the three terms is the interpreter; a second term is the object—the person or the meaning or the text—which is interpreted; the third is the person to whom the interpretation is addressed. (287)

Once an interpreter enters into the hermeneutic moment, the sign, as the outward dimension of the interpretation, becomes changed and articulated in the light of real and possible interpretees. As each new interpretee becomes an interpreter, the sign receives further elaboration and analysis. This process can continue indefinitely.

Extending the triadic model to self-knowledge, we see the present self looking on its past self as a sign to be interpreted to its future self. The future self thus functions as the interpretee. This temporal stretch complicates the problem of self-identity in that the present self can never claim to have arrived at the final and indubitable self-image.

For example, suppose the present self discovers that in the past it made a written promise to honor a certain social relation such as the agreement to serve in a branch of the military. Suppose further that intervening events have caused the present self to reject its previous commitment in the light of a projected future self or self-image. The triadic logic of interpretation has the task of illuminating this complex relation. Just who is this past self, and how compelling is its commitment in the light of changed attitudes? Can the present self simply claim that a radical conversion (Sartre) has taken place and that all contracts from the past are canceled? Can the hoped-for future self alter the very perception of the past so as to show obligations in a new light? The problem of moral obligation obviously becomes more difficult when the temporal element becomes central to an analysis of self-identity.

The problem of personal and communal identity is further complicated when it is realized that the process of sign manipulation is endless. A particular interpretation may fade from view, but the process itself continues. No sign is totally self-explanatory. Further articulation is always possible and, so Peirce would insist, necessary. The process of further articulation makes signs at least potentially social. Royce states,

> Peirce uses the term "sign" to name this mental object which is interpreted. Thirdly, since the interpretation is a mental act, and is an act which is expressed, the interpretation itself is, in its turn, a Sign. This new sign calls for further interpretation. For the interpretation is addressed to somebody. And so,—at least in ideal,—the social process involved is endless. (289-90)

A given sign is given to an interpretee who in turn will pass the sign on to another individual. A sign enriches its meaning in this transfer process, yet it retains its overall contour as long as the community works carefully to avoid arbitrary and destructive interpretations.

Taking a brief sidetrack, we can see how Royce elaborated the triadic schema in relation to problems in the philosophy of mind. In 1916 Royce published an article entitled "Mind" in the *Encyclopedia of Religion and Ethics*. In it he works out once again his general epistemology as it relates to the problem of interpretation.

As he did in *The Problem of Christianity*, Royce contrasts two types of knowledge as they have been articulated by the tradition. The first — conceptual knowledge, or "knowledge about"—he attributes to Plato. This is abstract categorial knowledge about general and pervasive structures. The second—perceptual knowledge, or "knowledge by acquaintance"—he attributes to James and Bergson.[7] Royce denies that either form is sufficient unto itself. Not only are all general concepts loaded with intuitive content, but all perceptions have some degree of generality, or thirdness. When we come to the more complex realms of self-knowledge or social knowledge, this simple binary model breaks down completely. Reiterating his Peircean epistemology, Royce argues,

> Every case of social intercourse between man and man, or (what is still more important) every process of inner self-comprehension carried on when a man endeavours to "make up his own mind" or "to understand what he is about," involves this third type of cognition, which cannot be reduced to perception or to conception. It is this third cognitive process that, following the terminology which Peirce proposed, we here apply the name "interpretation."[8]

There cannot be a "piece" of knowledge that is simply perceptual or conceptual. Both are ingredients in the act of interpretation itself. At this point, an interesting problem emerges, namely, how are we to isolate the moments within the act of interpretation? That is, if we must have both perception and conception in a hermeneutic act, just how do we know when we have passed from one to another? Strictly, Royce's theory does not call for this distinction from within a given interpretive act. Yet if we are to retain some minimal sense of the two terms in the dyad, we must find some means of telling them apart. Royce argues that this distinction can be drawn in theory but that it is extremely difficult to make it consistently in practice. We can sense that a given interpretation or sign has a greater degree of perception or a greater degree of conception, but it would be impossible for finite mind to determine the exact degree of each. We clearly do not first have a perception that then finds a conception later in a temporal sequence. Both emerge together. The triadic model occupies a curious position midway between a phenomenological account and a more formal transcendental argument that moves from what is the case to what must be the case for something to obtain.

---

[7]Josiah Royce, *Basic Writings*, 2 vols., ed. John J. McDermott (Chicago: University of Chicago Press, 1969) 2:736.

[8]Ibid., 741.

Without solving this problem, we can deepen our grasp of Royce's general framework by noting that he addresses this dyadic tension by indirectly referring to Bertrand Russell's own theory of knowledge. Russell was teaching at Harvard during the spring semester in 1914, and Royce expressed great admiration for his mind and philosophical ability.[9] One of Russell's courses was on the theory of knowledge, and he there presented his famous distinction between "knowledge by description" and "knowledge by acquaintance," which attempts to show the difference between mediated/conceptual knowledge and immediate perceptual knowledge. Royce, again writing in the 1916 article "Mind," is critical of this distinction.

> Interpretation is the knowledge of the meaning of a sign. Such a knowledge is not a merely immediate apprehension, not yet a merely conceptual process; it is the essentially social process whereby the knower at once distinguishes himself, with his own meanings, ideas, and expressions, from some other self, and at the same time knows that these selves have their conceptual meanings, while one of them at the moment is expressing its meaning to another. Knowledge by interpretation is, therefore, in its essence neither mere "acquaintance" nor yet "knowledge about."[10]

It should be clear that a sign is not a sense-datum and is far more complex in makeup. Russell's simple dyadic scheme denies the unity found in the interpretation and creates an abyss between the two forms of knowledge. Even if one were to add description and acquaintance together, no unified or social knowledge could emerge. The dyadic model creates difficulties that cannot be overcome.

In *The Problem of Christianity*, Royce expands upon his theory of interpretation by redefining philosophy itself. He states, "Interpretation is, once for all, the main business of philosophy" (297). Philosophy itself, as it functions to make clear the conditions under which interpretation can take place, can be seen to be equivalent to the general science of hermeneutics. Furthermore, as should be clear, philosophy is normative in its efforts to legislate the conditions under which interpretation should take place. The most general normative horizon is that of the community of interpretation as it mediates the wealth of thirds.

Royce links the use of thirds to the very basic mental act of finding comparisons and differences between and among realities.

> Thus a complete act of comparison involves such a "third," such a "mediating" image or idea,—such as "interpreter." By means of this "third" you so compare a "first" object with a "second" as to make clear to your-

---

[9]Royce to Ralph Barton Perry, 11 Feb. 1913, in Josiah Royce, *Letters*, ed. John Clendenning (Chicago: University of Chicago Press, 1970) 591-92.

[10]Royce, *Basic Writings*, 2:743.

self wherein consists the similarity and the difference between the second and the first. Comparison must be triadic in order to be both explicit and complete. Likenesses and differences are the sign that a comparison is needed. But these signs are not their own interpretation. (300)

Thirds function to preserve and present identity and difference in the complexes that are examined by the community of interpretation. Thus these interpretive thirds are doing ontological labor. Royce insists that these thirds may function as pragmatic leading ideas that unify inquiry by giving us a stable basis for making predictions. Yet thirds can also play a much larger role by providing the general horizon within which interpretations of lesser scope may appear.

Thirds can emerge in a number of ways. Like Peirce, Royce rejects the facile model of knowledge stemming from simplistic and positivistic understandings of scientific inquiry. Thirds can emerge from deduction, induction, abduction, and a process of musement. The latter two processes need not be lineal or directed toward specific goals. A certain randomness is appropriate when generating leading ideas of a high degree of generality. Royce states, "Now in the individual case, an interpretation, a mediating idea, may come to mind through almost any play of association, or as the result of almost any degree of skill in invention, or as the outcome either of serious or of playful combination" (310). One can find a mediating idea purely by accident or by the free actions of imaginative association. The source is not as important as the projected outcome. The mediating thirds will be tested by the general community in its quest for ultimate intelligibility. Standing behind the given community of interpretation is an ideal observer who functions as the guarantor of given interpretations. This observer is akin to the Absolute of his earlier writing.

The eventual goal of our interpretive activity is the production of the Beloved Community, which functions to unite these hermeneutic acts through the spirit of loyalty. Royce now links together two strands of his perspective. The Beloved Community is the Universal Church, which stands, at least initially, as the body of Christ. Yet this hoped-for community is also the community of interpretation. We can thus conclude that the Beloved Community of the first half of *The Problem of Christianity* is the inner telos of the community of interpretation of the second half. Royce brings these two notions together as follows:

When Christianity teaches us to hope for the community of all mankind, we can readily see that the Beloved Community, whatever else it is, will be, when it comes, a Community of Interpretation. When we consider the ideal form and the goal of such a community, we see that in no other form, and with no other ideal, can we better express the constitution of the ideal Church, be that conceived as the Church on earth or as the Church triumphant in some ideal realm of super-human and all seeing insight, where I shall know even as I am known. (318)

The "Church triumphant" would be the kingdom in which all hermeneutic acts receive immediate confirmation and seal. It is the realm "where
I shall know even as I am known." The goal of philosophy is thus the invisible church, which serves as the final telos of our hermeneutic acts. To
interpret is to strive to see the world as God sees it and as we would see
it in the ideal kingdom.

While the community of interpretation is more generic than the Beloved Community (that is, more exemplified in human life), it is still underway toward that loyal community in which all persons will be assured
of atonement and peace. Christ stands at the head of the hoped-for Beloved Community and guarantees membership to all who overcome the
self-will and rise to the demands of loyalty.

In an interesting passage, Royce combines his Pauline insights (to be
discussed in detail later) with his nondyadic theory of knowledge.

> Pragmatism, whose ideas, like those of the bewitched Galatians, are fain
> to be saved by their own "works," is, as I believe, quite unable to define
> in its own dyadic terms, the essentially spiritual sense in which any inter-
> pretation can be true, and the sense in which any community of interpre-
> tation could reach its goal. (329)

Paul is thus understood to have criticized the Galatians along the same
lines as a modern idealist would criticize pragmatists. Both advocate a form
of "works righteousness" as the way to salvation and truth. Pragmatism
uses the dyadic mode, in which a leading idea is applied to some percept
so as to ensure knowledge. Royce advocates an absolutistic pragmatism
that avoids the subjectivism and dualism of the kind of pragmatism prac-
ticed by William James.

With his understanding of the community of interpretation, his definition of reality should not come as a surprise.

> We all of us believe that there is any real world at all, simply because
> we find ourselves in a situation in which, because of the fragmentary and
> dissatisfying conflicts, antitheses, and the problems of our present ideas,
> an interpretation of this situation is needed, but it is not now known by us.
> By the "real world" we mean simply the "true interpretation" of this our
> problematic situation. (337)

The "real world" is not yet known to us, but when it does become known
by the Beloved Community, it will be the "true interpretation" of our situation. This "true interpretation" will be that which corresponds to the
mind and vision of God as that God is manifest in the community.

The community of interpretation is the horizon through which our various interpretations and signs are filtered on their way toward validation.
As noted above, the notion of the Absolute becomes transformed into the
notion of the living Spirit that stands behind the interpretations of the community. By putting community at the center of his later perspective, Royce
gave greater concreteness to the actual process of interpretation.

By stressing community over against an atemporal Absolute, Royce can overcome the sterility of monism, which insists on one and only one interpretation of "this our problematic situation." His commitment to pluralism is not often noted or appreciated. By stressing both community and the legitimacy of regional differences, Royce allows for more than one interpretation of the world. While God seems to be lurking behind the scenes, one senses that the real stress is on the community of interpretation as it struggles to validate signs.

Signs are to be found wherever persons interpret reality. This insight is a generalization of Peirce's semiotics in that signs are seen to be the way the world becomes understood. Without a sign there can be no knowledge. With a sign or sign series the individual can communicate with another and contrast and compare interpretations. Semiotics, as understood by Royce, is in the service of communication. The communication process itself is facilitated by the structure of the signs being communicated. Signs convey the unique category of thirdness. This category is crucial to both epistemology and metaphysics. Royce restates Peirce's analysis of signs as follows:

> Peirce insists that the signs, viewed simply from a logical point of view, constitute a new and fundamentally important category. He sets this category as a "third," side by side with the classic categories of the "universals" which form the "first" category, and the "individuals," which, in Peirce's logic, form the "second" category. (345)

The universality conveyed by firsts is not the same as that conveyed by thirds. Firsts convey qualitative integrity and unity but do not generate intelligible or conscious universals. True general thirds present conceptual generals that can be articulated in some form of utterance and that can be conveyed through social communication. To interpret is to seek to find the generic trait that is carried by the sign under study. Both Peirce and Royce, as realists on the universals problem, believe that thirdness is real and that it depicts generals in nature itself. Both thinkers are idealists, however, in that they stress the centrality of consciousness in grasping and framing signs and their universal elements. It should be emphasized that, while both thinkers are indebted to the critical turn of Kant, neither would go so far as to assume that nature is little more than a chaotic manifold in need of human categorial projections. Signs and thirds are embedded in a reality that transcends human consciousness, even though that reality requires consciousness for its full articulation.

Royce insists that we also need a proper attitude of will if we are to live within the interpretive community. We must reject any attitude that works against the hermeneutic process and its concern with signs and thirds. An attitude to be rejected is that embodied by the philosopher Schopenhauer. Royce correctly understands the general ontology of Schopenhauer to be one that stresses the priority of the unbridled and unguided will to live. This will to live is found in all beings and forces them to struggle against each other for domination. This force gives rise to a tragic struggle that, in its extreme forms, makes community impossible.

There is, however, an attitude of will that does serve the general hermeneutic process of communal query—the attitude of genuine (not natural) loyalty. One must love (be loyal to) the entire universe and all the interpreters in it. The loyal will enables the finite interpreter to subsume his or her will to the interpretive direction of the community. Genuine loyalty is both articulate and strenuous. Once again Royce returns to Paul to formalize his views on loyalty.

> The attitude of the will which Paul found to be saving in its power, just as, to his mind, it was also divine in its origin, was the attitude of Loyalty. Now loyalty, when considered from within, and with respect to its deepest spirit, is not the affirmation of the will to live of which Schopenhauer spoke. And loyalty is not the denial of the will to live. It is a positive devotion of the Self to its cause,—a devotion as vigorous, as self-asserting, as articulate, as strenuous, as Paul's life and counsels always remained. (356)

Without this loyalty we could not have a community, and without a community we could not have interpretations. Interpretations require communal articulation and ramification. These articulations are part of the sign series that unfolds through time and across provinces of meaning. The totality of these signs and their attendant meanings form the substance of our known world.

Returning to the specific view of reality emergent from the community of interpretation, we can see that the world is constituted by the community and its signs. According to Royce,

> Our doctrine of Signs extends to the whole world the same fundamental principle. The World is the Community. The world contains its own interpreter. Its processes are infinite in their temporal varieties. But their interpreter, the spirit of the universal community,—never absorbing varieties or permitting them to blend,—compares, and through a real life, interprets them all. (362)

This is a strong metaphysical claim. To be is to be part of a community that has its own interpreter. To be part of a community is to be a sign series in the process of constant transformation. Hence self-identity is derived from a series of hermeneutic acts that collectively serve to show the contour of the self. Passing beyond persons, we can see the rest of reality as the product of an unbounded (infinite) series of hermeneutic acts. Reality, then, is the ideal future interpretation of our "problematic situation."

Christianity is seen as the religion that comes closest to grasping both the nature of reality and the actual path (loyalty) to the cognition of that reality.

> The essential message of Christianity has been the word that the sense of life, the very being of the time process itself, consists in the progressive

realization of the Universal Community in and through the longings, the
vicissitudes, the tragedies, and the triumphs of this process in the temporal world. (387)

From our more specific Beloved Community we can hope to build toward
the Universal Community, in which all persons will contribute to the
general hermeneutic process of finding the true interpretations of reality.
There are indeed many signs that we can hope for such a Universal Community. Royce believes that the community of science gives us one such
sign that interpreters can unite together around a common body of signs
and that they can hope to universalize their knowledge.

For Royce, the very existence of the sciences demonstrates that the
universe has an interpreter. In the evolution of consciousness, humans
have attained distance from the immediacy with nature, which has enabled them to find general truths. The movement from the arts of simple
hunting and planting to the chemical analysis of matter is one involving
a steady utilization of social signs. This process has been a progressive
one in which our original ignorance of natural processes has given way
to a deeper sense of the traits of organic and inorganic orders. The semiotic transformation of knowledge has not taken us away from nature
but, through social communication, has brought us closer to its secrets
than would have been possible otherwise.

The spirit of the scientific community, however, especially as presented by Peirce, is not alone sufficient for the emergence of the Universal Community. Royce insists that only the addition of the spirit of Christ
can ensure that signs move toward transparency and convergence in the
ideal future. Christology needs to be transformed so as to go beyond static
doctrines of the nature of the Christ. Rather, we must see Christology as
our practical commitment that responds in deeds to the Spirit's call toward preaching the Beloved and Universal Communities. This is following the real Christ. Royce asserts,

> What is practically necessary is therefore this: Let your Christology be
> the practical acknowledgment of the Spirit of the Universal and Beloved
> Community. This is the sufficient and practical faith. Love this faith, use
> this faith, teach this faith, preach this faith, in whatever words, through
> whatever symbols, by means of whatever forms of creeds, in accordance
> with whatever practices best you find to enable you with a sincere intent
> and a whole heart to symbolize and to realize the presence of the Spirit in
> the community. (403-404)

Hence the more traditional role of Christology as the foundation for church
doctrine about the second person of the Trinity is replaced by this active
and social role. Christ, in his person as Jesus, is pushed into the background so that the doctrine of the community and its animating Spirit-
Interpreter may become central.

Royce concludes the second half of *The Problem of Christianity* by re-
stating the general views of Christ and community as they were devel-

oped in the first half. Above all, he stresses the role of the Spirit in making the community viable.

> The core, the center of the faith, is not the person of the individual foun-
> der, and is not any other individual man. Nor is this core to be found in
> the sayings of the founder, nor yet in the traditions of Christology. The core
> of the faith is the Spirit, the Beloved Community, the work of grace, the
> atoning deed, and the saving power of the loyal life. There is nothing else
> under heaven whereby men have been saved or can be saved. To say this
> is to found no new faith, but to send you to the heart of all true faith. (404)

His position remains at the opposite pole from theological liberalism, which insists on the person and life of Jesus as the essence of the faith. Rather, the ethic and religion of loyalty, as derived from Paul and his own earlier work, become the keys to the kingdom. Outside of this Beloved Community the individual could not hoped to be saved.

By now it should be evident that all of these elements combine to produce a general and fruitful philosophical hermeneutics. Such a hermeneutics has as its concern the interpretation of all reality and the presentation of the series of interpretations in a body of signs. Royce not only shows how the individual engages in interpretive acts but goes much further by showing how these acts must exist within the community of interpretation. This community forms the interpretive horizon within which any sign must receive its determination and validation. The individual interpreter is a community in microcosm in that he or she is constituted by a series of signs or self-images. Personal identity is thereby rendered as a social product and achievement.

Behind this social hermeneutics lies a general metaphysics that asserts that the universe consists of signs and their interpretations. Royce posits an ideal interpreter as the guarantor of our hermeneutic acts. This ideal interpreter, operating outside of the horizon of the community, satisfies our phenomenological need for divine validation. Through its spiritual presence we move toward the Beloved Community, in which all signs will become transparent in their meaning.

In the pre-1912 framework the Absolute is envisioned as an atemporal self that is fully self-conscious. This Absolute has many traits in common with Aristotle's *Nous*. After 1912, Royce's Absolute appears as the agent Spirit that functions to quicken Christian social praxis. Specifically, the Spirit is the Spirit of Interpretation that gently moves the community toward hermeneutic convergence. The Spirit aids the individual toward interpretations that will preserve and further the needs of the Universal Community.

The community is the horizon within which hermeneutics moves. Outside of the Spirit-filled community, diremption and distortion govern the life of interpretation. Royce's semiotics works hand in hand with his reconstruction of Pauline Christianity to show how hermeneutics derives its validation and power. Our appropriation of this legacy must remain attuned to his reworking of Peirce and to his sensitive understanding of the community as the body of Christ. At the same time, we must move toward a horizonal hermeneutics that avoids some of the excesses of Royce's idealism (see chapter 3).

LANGUAGE MYSTICISM IN THE CONTINENTAL HERMENEUTICS OF GADAMER AND HEIDEGGER

Recent work in hermeneutic theory on the Continent has tended to stress the finite self in its private relation to a text or utterance. Out of this relation has emerged a concern for the hermeneutic horizon that governs the interpretive transaction between the self and the artifact. By framing the hermeneutic problem in this fashion, Continental thinkers have limited the scope both of the agent of interpretation and of the object. This limitation has in turn forced hermeneutic theory into a subjective and nongeneric structure. The interpretive burden is placed on the acts of fusion by and through which one historical horizon becomes binding for another. These acts of fusion themselves are the provenance of the individual and fall outside of the quest for communal validation. As a result of this subjective delineation of the problem, hermeneutic theory remains unable to emancipate itself from the sphere of privacy.

Royce's mature reflections on the nature of the hermeneutic act and its proper location within the evolving community of interpretation provide a framework that overcomes the distortions of the hermeneutic theories of Gadamer and Heidegger. As we saw in chapter 1, the community of interpretation is the horizon through which our various interpretations and signs are filtered on their way to eventual validation. Royce's pre-1912 notion of the Absolute is transformed into the temporal realm of the community as guided by the Spirit. The semiotic triad of antecedent, present, and hoped-for sign forms the mechanism for smooth sign translation for both the individual and the community. Each individual achieves both internal and external semiotic transparency only through the constant sign translation that forms the living body of the community. Hence the community and not the self forms the horizon for each hermeneutic act. The general interpretive horizons that constitute personal perspective are all products of communal ramification and articulation. The community of interpretation is thus both the horizon and the source of horizons for all hermeneutic acts. Outside of this horizon no knowledge claims can hope to have validation or enrichment.

At this point we are ready to make explicit comparisons between the mature Roycean view and those of Gadamer and Heidegger. Of initial importance is the concept of horizon itself. This notion emerged in the work of Husserl as a way of dealing with the surrounding phenomenal field of our intentional acts. Yet the hermeneutic understanding of horizon emerged more fully with the work of Hans-Georg Gadamer. He defines horizon in his major work, *Truth and Method*, as

> not a rigid frontier, but something that moves with one and invites one to advance further. Thus horizon intentionality, which constitutes the unity of the flow of experience, is paralleled by an equally comprehensive horizon intentionality on the objective side. For everything that is given as existent is given in terms of the world and hence brings the world horizon with it.[1]

Both subject and object belong within the intentional structures of a moving and open horizon. The horizon must not be seen as a closed totality that is fully determined. Rather, it is something that lures us beyond ourselves into larger stretches of experience and world encounter.

Another way of understanding the concept of horizon is in terms of the notion of perspective. A perspective is not merely a subjective coloring of reality that we can somehow enter into at will. Rather, a perspective, like a horizon, is something larger than the subject. It occupies a domain between the subject and its objects and preserves the open region within which they can encounter each other. Justus Buchler, partially working out of a dialogue with Peirce and Royce, rethinks the nature of perspectives in a way that is not unlike Gadamer's account of horizon.

> A perspective is a kind of order, that kind of order in which a given set of natural complexes function [*sic*] as procepts for a given proceiver or (distributively) for a community of proceivers. To say that different proceivers share the same perspective is to say that the order in which each is related to a class of procepts is one and the same order. But some relations or orders are unique and unrepeated, even though they are, in part, of a common and repeatable character, and an instance of such an order would be the proceptive domain itself.[2]

For Buchler, a perspective is a "humanly occupied order" that has a direction and a meaning beyond given conscious intents. Natural complexes, his term for "whatever is in whatever way," function as procepts

---

[1] Hans-Georg Gadamer, *Truth and Method* (New York: Seabury Press, 1975) 217.

[2] Justus Buchler, *Toward a General Theory of Human Judgment,* 2d rev. ed. (New York: Dover Publications, 1979) 124-25.

for the individual or the community. A procept is a natural complex as it relates to a proceiver (roughly, an object of experience as it relates to the individual). Thus a perspective is that which governs the way natural complexes are "experienced." We can have a common (or parallel) perspective insofar as two or more proceivers jointly assimilate and manipulate the same natural complexes. We can have different perspectives insofar as we cannot repeat or share our procepts. Buchler, largely under the impress of Peirce and Royce, sees the community as the place where perspectives are shared and communicated.

Both horizons and perspectives govern the ways in which the world is seen or otherwise rendered available for human probing and possible sign translation. Each can be either private or held in common. Both the horizon and the perspective transcend that which is conscious or clear and distinct. For Gadamer, we can have a fusion of horizons, while for Buchler, perspectives are amenable to translation and comparison. Within a given horizon or perspective a certain order obtains, however minimal, and this order governs the ways in which horizonal and perspectival intersections occur. Futhermore, each semiotic addition to a horizon or perspective is governed by the internal structures of the parent framework.

More specifically, we can say that a horizon (perspective) has both temporal and spatial traits. As temporal, the horizon is a felt continuity with the past and an expectation for the future. Royce's "community of memory" and "community of expectation" function in just this manner. As spatial, the horizon is extended across numerous signs (or, more generically, natural complexes) and represents the occupation of a domain. The spatial scope of the horizon grants and preserves place. The hermeneutic articulation of place is horizonal topology. As temporal, the horizon is the clearing within and through which what is can come to manifest appearance. The horizon (perspective) has both temporal and spatial scope and is constituted by both achieved and achievable meanings. Surrounding meanings had and hoped for are those that can never be made available to human community. Closure marks the boundary of any horizon—a penumbra that both grants and hides the light. Hence the horizon can never achieve total illumination. It stands as an encompassing measure that yet, in its fitful withdrawal, allows meaning.

Horizons are not self-contained monads but must, often with tragic urgency, interact with other horizons. For Gadamer, this process is known as fusion. In horizonal fusion the various modes of time are brought together. In one dimension, fusion involves the temporal aspects of a given horizon. In another dimension it involves the reach across horizons to generate and sustain horizonal intersection. Concerning the temporal dimension of fusion, Gadamer states,

> In fact the horizon of the present is being continually formed, in that we have continually to test all our prejudices. An important part of this testing is the encounter with the past and the understanding of the tradition from

which we come. Hence the horizon of the present cannot be formed without the past. There is no more an isolated horizon of the present than there are historical horizons. Understanding, rather, is always the fusion of these horizons which we imagine to exist by themselves.[3]

The analysis of horizons in terms of temporal spread and fusion is remarkably similar to that of Royce. The concept of the community of interpretation involves the presence of both the felt past of common (and heroic) deeds and hoped-for consummation in an ideal future (in the grace-filled Beloved Community). No so-called present horizon can function without the copresence of past and future. Tradition forms the evolving matrix, which itself functions as a lure, for each present assimilation and manipulation of signs and complexes. Fusion, for both Royce and Gadamer, is a phenomenological given of individual life. For Royce, of course, fusion is also constitutive of communal transactions.

In the second dimension, fusion entails the copenetration of alien orders. Royce's 1908 article on provincialism entails that a given perspective will have built-in meaning parameters that govern or direct the manner of fusion. In other words, the beliefs (Gadamer's *Vorurteilen*, "prejudices") of one province can be brought into intersection (fusion) with those of another. In the process neither province is forced to lose all of its unique elements. The result is greater semiotic spread for both provinces. Yet no overarching horizon of horizons will come to dominate all provincial horizons. The integrity of each will be preserved, even while the scope increases.

For Buchler, perspectives are translatable into each other, even though this process can never produce strict one-to-one correspondence. Perspectives are at least partially unique. "All perspectives may be called irreducible, however, in the sense that they are distinctive; and by definition, that which is distinctive or unique cannot be translated into another which is exactly equivalent, though of course it can be 'translated' in the important sense of being rendered available."[4] To render "available" is to make a perspective function as part of a newer and larger perspective. That is, the elements in the perspective can occupy important places in the more encompassing perspective. Thus, for example, the perspective known as primitive medicine can take on a new role (be rendered available) in the larger perspective of modern psychiatry. By becoming available in this way, the primitive forms become "translated" and reworked so as to serve the new perspective. In the process the internal semiotic structures of the primitive perspective are transformed so as to reveal a different transparency and meaning structure. Continuity and discontinuity prevail as the process deepens in complexity.

---

[3]Gadamer, *Truth and Method*, 273.

[4]Buchler, *Theory of Human Judgment*, 6.

The parallels to Royce should be evident. The community of interpretation functions as the horizon or perspective through which all signs pass on their way to interpretive transparency. The community of interpretation has both a felt past and hoped-for future of semiotic convergence. Furthermore, it has its own perspective, its own way of understanding the signs at its disposal. The perspective governs the process of serial ramification. No sign can remain free from the pressure of the dominant horizon or perspective that is the community of interpretation. The process of translation is the process of serial ramification whereby a given sign I becomes sign I ^{1}. On the higher level, when one entire perspective confronts the community of interpretation, we have to deal with whole sign series as they function in an alien environment.

Royce and Gadamer part company when they respectively treat the objects of hermeneutic determination. Gadamer, under the impress of Heidegger, sees language as the essential expression of meaning in our finite situation.[5] Language is the proper object of our hermeneutic acts because in language our being-in-the-world is most fully expressed. This form of "language mysticism" harks back to the hermeneutic program of the liberal theologian Schleiermacher, for whom the written document stands as the external expression of the internal mental evolution of the author. Given Gadamer's harsh criticism of Schleiermacher, this ironic parallel should not pass without our notice. The turn toward language functions in both Schleiermacher and Gadamer to limit the generic power of the general framework. Gadamer expresses the centrality of language as follows:

> The occasionality of human speech is not a casual imperfection of its expressive power; it is, rather, the logical expression of the virtuality of speech, that brings a totality of meaning into play, without being able to express it totally. All human speaking is finite in such a way that there is within it an infinity of meaning to be elaborated and interpreted. That is why the hermeneutical phenomenon also can be illuminated only in the light of this fundamental finitude of being, which is wholly linguistic in character.[6]

Our finitude can come to expression only in speech acts. Gadamer places the stress not so much on the product as on the speaking. Yet the emphasis is still on the utter centrality of language as the carrier of meaning.

---

[5]In Heidegger's reflections on language, three stages can be distinguished: the first, in *Sein und Zeit*, where he distinguishes between authentic discourse (*Rede*) and idle talk or inauthentic discourse (*Gerede*); the second, in the 1930s, where he speaks of language as *Sprache*; and finally, in the 1950s, where he speaks of language as saying, or saga (*Sage*). The differentia between discourse, authentic or otherwise, speaking, and saying must be kept in view to obtain an adequate grasp of Heidegger's hermeneutic of language.

[6]Gadamer, *Truth and Method*, 416.

While language can "express" the inexpressible, it remains the locus of attained meanings. Language is best understood, according to Gadamer, as finite human speech.

Royce would reply that meaning can be conveyed by any sign. A sign need not be expressed or expressible in language. To go back to Peirce, an iconic sign need show only its common structural or pictorial form with its referent in order to convey meaning. Of course, in Royce's 1913 appropriation of Peirce's semiotics, the division of signs into icons, indexes, and symbols is not carried over into the hermeneutics. Yet such a general extension of sign structures outside of natural human speech was envisioned by Royce. Any artifact or gesture can convey semiotic meaning. The orders of nature are more than ripe with analogical and indexical meanings. Hence, meaning need not be limited to the order of human utterance. Any complex can function as a sign insofar as it impacts on human awareness in meaningful ways.

In what many might see as an advance beyond Peirce, Royce recasts semiotics in such a way as to downplay the reference relation in order to broaden our understanding of the spectrum of responses in the sign relation. Buchler sketches this divergence as follows: "Royce and Mead, though not so aware as Peirce of the possible complexities of the sign-relation, sensed the greater importance of interpretation or response in the sign-relation and the lesser importance of the sign as a designation, a vehicle of reference."[7]

The emphasis on the *response* to the sign or sign series gives Royce's semiotics a more dramatic flavor than that found in Peirce's writings. By moving away from a precise delineation of the reference function, Royce was able to give greater articulation to the semiotic process of triadic progression in the unfolding of serial meaning. The response patterns (habits of mental life) found in the community of interpretation govern the scope of both meaning and possible reference for each sign. We can say that the reference is a secondary act that functions in a general teleology of convergent validation. By shifting the burden of semiotic theory in this direction, Royce made a bold advance beyond Peirce, while at the same time placing his general conclusions on a more secure foundation than that which emerged out of the work of Gadamer. This advance is noted by Karl-Otto Apel in his book on Peirce. "Royce's idea of the 'community of interpreters,' expounded in the second volume of his last work, *The Problem of Christianity* (1913), provides perhaps the most important single contribution to the extension and development in hermeneutic and social philosophical terms of Peirce's semiotic."[8] By recasting semiotics and in

---

[7]Justus Buchler, *Nature and Judgment* (New York: Columbia University Press, 1955) 155-66.

[8]Karl-Otto Apel, *Charles S. Peirce: From Pragmatism to Pragmaticism*, trans. John Michael Krois (Amherst: University of Massachusetts Press, 1981) 135.

turn grafting it onto the horizon of the community, Royce gave greater scope to the object of hermeneutics. His rethinking of the nature of the self as a sign series in need of communal contrast is of a piece with his extension of semiotics beyond the reference function. Both revisions enhanced the generic power of his hermeneutic theory.

Since anything can function as a sign, there is no theoretical need to isolate one type or genus of signs as being fundamental in all respects. The "language mysticism" of Gadamer and Heidegger imposes a priority scheme that reduces the status of nonlinguistic sign meanings. For Heidegger, language exists as the primal Saying that calls forth all beings into presence. Outside of this evocation, beings are condemned to remain hidden. Furthermore, Saying calls forth the presence itself that is conveyed in the word *Being* (*das Sein*). Like Gadamer, Heidegger assumes that only language in its speaking (Saying) can present and preserve meaning. In his 1959 essay "The Way to Language," he states,

> Language first of all and inherently obeys the essential nature of speaking: it says. Language speaks by saying, that is, by showing. What it says wells up from the formerly spoken and so far still unspoken Saying which pervades the design of language. Language speaks in that it, as showing, reaches into all regions of presences, summons from them whatever is present to appear and to fade. We, accordingly, listen to language in this way, that we let it say its Saying to us.[9]

Our relation to language is, in one sense at least, passive. We listen to the ways in which language itself speaks. True language (namely, Saying) forms the "House of Being" through which and in which beings can appear in the fitful light of Being. Hermeneutics becomes the art of letting Saying gather us into the Appropriation that holds Being and mortals together in cotransparency. Saying grants us our very place in the world and lets meaning become present to us.

At no point can the individual listener appeal to a larger community in order to test and validate that which Saying evokes and provokes. Heidegger, as has often been said, cuts off all possible relation to a living community that would serve to filter the oracular sayings of language. The very idea of validation is held to be alien to true Thinking, which is primarily a listening to the mittances of primal Being.

Heidegger is, of course, correct when he criticizes the conception of language that stresses the exclusively denotative function of terms. Only a conception rooted in the paradigm of the noun, which in turn rejects verbal and gerundial functions, can see the sentence (proposition) as constituted by simple one-to-one reference to an independent state of affairs. Indeed, Wittgenstein moved to the same insight in rejecting his own

---

[9]Martin Heidegger, *On the Way to Language*, trans. Peter Hertz and Joan Stambaugh (New York: Harper & Row, 1971) 124.

earlier picture model of the proposition. Heidegger has, as is well known, a deeper reason for rejecting a purely denotative conception of language, namely, the desire to preserve our authentic relation to beings. In his 1935 lectures on metaphysics Heidegger states, "Words and language are not wrappings in which things are packed for the commerce of those who write and speak. It is in words and language that things first come into being and are. For this reason the misuse of language in idle talk (*Gerede*), in slogans and phrases, destroys our authentic relation to things."[10]

Idle talk casts a veil of semblance over the pristine emergence of the things in our environment. Our own inauthentic existence drags language downward into the very flattened realm of information and unreflected thinking. The hermeneutic problem is tied irrevocably to the problem of personal authenticity. In authentic existence, however fitfully present in time, language is rescued from the decay that fuels mere curiosity and boredom. In this movement toward authenticity (which occurs in the early and later Heidegger), beings are allowed the pristine showing that can come only from a renewed relation to language. Language, as the "House of Being," becomes the gathering-clearing through which, for authentic Dasein, beings become what they are.

Language, as the site of meaning, functions as a gathering in which beings and their meanings are brought into fundamental relation and belonging. In the same 1935 lectures Heidegger states, "Because the essence of language is found in the act of gathering within the togetherness of being, language as everyday speech comes into its truth only when speaking and hearing are oriented toward logos as collectedness in the sense of being."[11] Truth, as the coming-into-presence of beings, emerges from the gathering presented and preserved in language. Untruth prevails when language is no longer attuned to the gathering of logos but stands outside of such a prethematic horizon. When proper speaking is attuned to proper hearing, the truth of the gathering can become manifest. Language can no longer be seen as the lineal carrier of discrete meanings and references. Rather, language is the shrine within which we recapture our belonging to the gathering of meaning that transcends our human projects.

This radical rethinking of the nature of language and meaning forces Heidegger to deconstruct what he understands as the tradition of metaphysics in Western philosophy. Metaphysics emerged as a separate discipline when Plato turned away from the primal notion of truth as presence to his doctrine of the Forms, in which being becomes the merely correct. Language, whether Greek, Latin, or modern, has been captured

---

[10]Martin Heidegger, *An Introduction to Metaphysics*, trans. Ralph Manheim (New Haven: Yale University Press, 1959) 13-14.

[11]Ibid., 173.

in the vortex of metaphysical and representational thinking that concerns itself with beings in terms of mere generic traits or of a highest being. The light of Being has been in eclipse since the beginning of philosophy proper and is now at the stage of deepest darkness. The crisis of nihilism (hardly an experience for Peirce or Royce) shows us just how far we have fallen from the pre-Socratic evocation of presence. In the poetic thinking envisioned by Heidegger, we can bring ourselves into the position to recall that which has fled from the West. Or rather, we can let ourselves be gathered into the withdrawal of Being so as to stand in this withdrawal in a fateful manner.

The nihilism of our epoch entails a crisis in the nature of our hermeneutic acts. If the source of meaning is in eclipse, then it follows that our efforts to recapture meaning are vain unless we can earn the perspective that allows the ground of meaning to return. In the radical turn toward meditative (as opposed to calculative) thinking, Heidegger insists that meaning, as preserved in the Saying of language, can return. The burden for this turning toward Being is placed on the shoulders of the solitary Thinker or poet who, because of a deeper relation to language, shows us the fateful path toward Being's unearned presence.

This privileging of the role of the poet makes all communal interpretive acts subaltern to the inaugural Saying that cannot admit of contrast and comparison. In his 1936 essay "Hölderlin and the Essence of Poetry," Heidegger gives language the status of a world-opening power.

> Language is not a mere tool, one of the many which man possesses; on the contrary, it is only language that affords the very possibility of standing in the openness of the existent. Only where there is language, is there world, i.e., the perpetually altering circuit of decision and production, of action and responsibility, but also of commotion and arbitrariness, of decay and confusion. Only where world predominates is there history. Language is a possession (*Gut*) in a more fundamental sense.[12]

World, as the totality of regions, shines forth through the primal utterances of the poet who brings the serenity of Being to those few for whom such insights are possible. The burden of language is great. On the one hand, it must be gathered into that which is now announcing its fateful withdrawal and respond to the draft created by Being's revocation. On the other hand, it must turn back toward the human and make both sides of the ontological difference (between Being and beings) transparent to the ever smaller community of poets and thinkers. This dual pressure brings language to the edge of its own self-annihilation.

The poet is not responsible for determining the contours of nature or of the world in its worlding. However, the poet takes on the deeper task

---

[12]Martin Heidegger, *Existence and Being*, ed. Werner Brock, essay as translated by Douglas Scott (Chicago: Regnery, 1949) 276.

of nominating the holy and those divinities who are granted their brief historical play through the light of the holy. In the same essay Heidegger states, "The poet names the gods and names all things in that which they are. This naming does not consist merely in something already known being supplied with a name; it is rather that when the poet speaks the essential word, the existent is by this naming nominated as what it is. So it becomes known as existent. Poetry is the establishing of being by means of the word."[13] Like Adam, the poet enables the existent (beings) to become unhidden and thereby to secure their place within the light of Being. The power of Being announces itself through the wording of the world and enables the poet to evoke the sense of place that makes true homecoming possible.

In his lecture "The Nature of Language," delivered in 1957-1958, Heidegger further explores the power of language to bring Being into its presence.

> If our thinking does justice to the matter, then we may never say of the word that it is, but that it gives—not in the sense that words are given by an "it," but that the word gives itself. The word itself is the giver. What does it give? To go by the poetic experience and by the most ancient tradition of thinking, the word gives Being. Our thinking, then, would have to seek the word, the giver which itself is never given, in this "there is that which gives."[14]

The word gives us Being by itself participating in the "it gives" (*es gibt*). This participation propels language into the realm in between the human and its fundamental ground. We are gathered into the word's derivative power and freed from our forgetfulness of Being. Once the word has overwhelmed us we can establish a community with Being. This relationship to the radiant light of that which is other than beings is the supposed source for the communality that relates us to those other mortals who are bereft of the light of Being. The language given to us by the poet is the primary opening to whatever community may be possible for those who are not part of the elect of Being.

The relation between the poet and those who use language as a mere tool is without interpretive interaction. There can be no symmetrical communication between those who stand on different sides of such an abyss. The poet is little more than the "place" where Being decides to let its presence be felt in the "it gives" of language. This mysticism of language closes off both the self and the community to any interpretive structures that might be shared and articulated in common. Ironically, Heidegger's drive for radical openness destroys the appearance of the ex-

---

[13]Ibid., 281.

[14]Heidegger, *On the Way to Language*, 88.

tralinguistic transactions that govern and define the human process. Interpretation is reduced to the poet's passive response to a voice that emerges from the other side of genuine community.

Royce would reply that all interpretation is interpretation for another (interpretee). It may appear to us that no such other is present (either potentially or actually), but we cannot fully grasp a sign or meaning until we enter into the triadic logic of sign translation, which itself is communal. Even if we were to admit that language is primarily the Saying of Being, we would still have to present that Saying in the communal structures of both awareness and utterance. The very fact that Heidegger has written extensively on the Saying of language shows that he is aware of the larger hermeneutic problem of effective communication. At the very least, Being must convey its traits to the finite interpreter through the kind of language that is tied to presence. Yet Heidegger remains bound to what Ricoeur calls a hermeneutics of the "I am." According to Ricoeur, "The kind of ontology developed by Heidegger gives ground to what I shall call a *hermeneutics of the 'I am,'* which is a repetition of the *cogito* conceived of as a simply epistemological principle."[15] Ironically, Heidegger returns to a form of substance mysticism in which the finite individual is forced to be the self-enfolded source and receptor of meaning in time. Given Heidegger's basic ontological delineations, he is unable to escape the sphere of privacy that has so vitiated the Cartesian trajectory in philosophy. Royce, in an advance beyond the type of thinking envisioned by the later Heidegger, not only admits the communal dimension but carefully exhibits its constitution and function. His semiotic redefinition of the self makes the communal dimension of meaning transparent in a fashion unavailable to Heidegger.

Returning to Buchler, we see that community is essential to any conveyance of knowledge. True communication is symmetrical in that it is shareable. It is asymmetrical, as understood by Royce, in that a sign translated is a sign changed. It is impossible to return to a sign before its transformation by other signs and interpretees. The symmetrical aspect of communication (its shareability) is described by Buchler.

> Symmetrical communication is both a requirement of animal survival and an avenue of abstract knowledge. It is both the condition of awareness and the fruit of awareness. It presupposes community, and community presupposes sharing. Now in order that community should obtain, it is necessary that some natural complex be a dominant procept for more than one individual in the same respect.[16]

---

[15] Paul Ricoeur, *The Conflict of Interpretations,* ed. Don Ihde (Evanston: Northwestern University Press, 1974) 223.

[16] Buchler, *Theory of Human Judgment,* 33.

Hence we cannot hope to have communication without community. As shown above, the community occupies a perspective, and this perspective (or perspectives) governs how signs or complexes will be interpreted. Furthermore, as not fully grasped by Heidegger, this communication must be symmetrical, with the interpretive process flowing from interpreter to interpretee. In doing so, it renders signs available for reinterpretation by the original interpreter, who receives an already transformed meaning from the interpretee.

Buchler's formulation comes closer to the Roycean model than does that of either Gadamer or Heidegger. Meanings conveyed must be articulated anew if they are to enter into the full scope of communal ramification. Royce's community of interpretation functions as the horizon or perspective that governs this process. It is a symmetrical process in that both interpreter and interpretee share in the constitution of meaning. It is an asymmetrical process in that one cannot go back from I^1 to I, for both temporal and interpretive reasons. Temporally, the past is altered in its translation into the present. Interpretively, a sign interpreted is a sign changed. We cannot erase either form of sign transformation. Hence the hermeneutic process is both symmetrical and asymmetrical, but in different respects.

Central to Gadamer's hermeneutics is the concern, akin to that of pragmatism, to unite practical and theoretical reason. Taking his cues from Aristotle, Gadamer links the hermeneutic process to the evolution of human understanding toward a practical evocation of the Good within the life of the community. Understanding is not limited to texts but drives toward interhuman communication. Rhetoric and dialectic receive their grounding in the hermeneutic process of discussion, which allows individuals to enter into horizons not their own. The modern notion of science fails to account for the social dimension of understanding. According to Gadamer,

> Social life consists of a constant process of transformation of what previously has been held valid. But it would surely be an illusion to want to deduce normative notions *in abstracto* and to posit them as valid with the claim of scientific rectitude. The point here is a notion of science that does not allow for the ideal of the nonparticipating observer but endeavors instead to bring to our reflective awareness the community that binds everyone together.[17]

Gadamer rejects the notion of a detached acommunal observer who would somehow rise up into the realm of a priori reflection. Our social interactions involve the dialectical interplay of the numerous prejudgments that guide rational reflection and speech. The various products of communi-

---

[17]Hans-Georg Gadamer, *Reason in the Age of Science*, trans. Frederick G. Lawrence (Cambridge: MIT Press, 1984) 135.

cation emerge at the termination of specific processes of dialogue and cannot be predicted beforehand as to their traits or eventual impact on the larger social order.

While the empirical sciences (the *Naturwissenschaften,* as opposed to the *Geisteswissenschaften*) rely upon specific methodologies, such as those of induction and abduction, hermeneutics remains an art of dialogic interaction that must feel the internal pressures of evolving forms of language. Any given discussion between two or more individuals will generate its own logic and rhythm, which cannot be foreclosed by a mechanical utilization of method. Understanding must wait upon the "right time" and not force human dialogue into predetermined patterns.

> Besides all that goes into knowledge (which ultimately includes everything knowable, or "the nature of the whole"), real knowledge has to recognize the *kairos.* This means knowing when and how one is required to speak. But this cannot be assimilated on one's own by way of rules and mere learning by rote. There are no rules governing the reasonable use of rules, as Kant stated so rightly in his *Critique of Judgment.*[18]

The moment of fulfilled time (the *kairos*) will emerge only when understanding moves beyond its obsession with empirical method and rises up into the movement of the speaking itself. The rudimentary beginnings of true communal existence emerge from the initial dialogue between finite individuals. Gadamer refers to Schleiermacher's romantic hermeneutics of personal friendship as having laid the historical foundation for his own notion of the understanding dialogue. In true friendship, individual horizons of meaning become open to each other so that horizonal plenitude may replace the narcissistic self-reference of precommunicative life.

Gadamer's insistence on the practical dimension of hermeneutics links him to the Roycean concern for the ethical transformation of the community. Royce's concept of loyalty to loyalty stands as the ethical forestructure for interpretation. We could paraphrase Royce by stating: interpret in a way that furthers the spirit of open-ended interpretation within the Beloved Community. Any hermeneutic act that would bring the interpretive process to a close is a disloyal act and must be atoned for by further interpreters. For Gadamer, each interpretation must point beyond its object, whether a text or an individual, and must illuminate something fundamental for social life. "Thinking always points beyond itself. Platonic dialogue has an expression for this; it refers to the one, the being, the good that presents itself in the order of the soul, the political constitution, or the nature of the world."[19] The Good, Royce's spirit of

---

[18]Ibid., 121.

[19]Hans-Georg Gadamer, *Philosophical Apprenticeships,* trans. Robert R. Sullivan (Cambridge: MIT Press, 1985) 186.

loyalty, emerges on the other side of our interpretive acts and gives them their meaning and direction. The practical dimension of understanding is the drive toward the unconditional source of value that keeps communal life from sinking into the demonic and nongeneric. Gadamer insists that the ethical core of dialogue saves hermeneutics from becoming a detached purview of mere structures. The drive to interpret is in essence the drive toward healthy social life.

The practical and social aspects of Gadamer's hermeneutics transcend the understanding of interpretation found in Heidegger. The isolated Dasein of Heidegger's *Sein und Zeit* remains unable to find a communal reality beyond the solitary reflections of a few thinkers and poets. Yet it does not follow that Gadamer has developed as rich a conceptual structure as that found in the later Royce. The movement of interpretation beyond given texts and individuals is a movement that is only potentially communal. One could argue that Royce's notion of community begins just where Gadamer's leaves off. The protocommunity found in Gadamer is, for Royce, a component within the individual and as such only partially communal. The "pointing beyond" of the given act of interpretation must be further located in the semiotic and hermeneutic structures of the community of interpretation. The value of Gadamer's perspective is that it brings us to the threshold of the larger communal view and thereby transcends the Heideggerian model.

Peirce and Royce each consider a theme that is of central importance for the hermeneutics of Gadamer (and in a more subtle form, for Heidegger). Peirce, in his discussion of methodology, introduced and exploited the idea of interpretive musement as a way of playfully manipulating meaning. This freestyle method is richer and more open than abduction and induction. Interpretive musement lifts the interpreter beyond the merely instrumental aspects of knowledge that normally characterize the problematic situation. Musement frees itself from a means/end structure and lets sign reflection unfold in directions not governed by the pressures of the immediate environment. Peirce's insight into semiotic musement enabled him to transcend traditional pragmatic accounts of the role of problem solving in stabilizing the organism in its surrounding world. Royce was also sensitive to this dimension of sign articulation and rejected mechanical methods that would deaden the novel elements in sign series. For Gadamer, the rough equivalent to interpretive musement is play (*Spiel*). As is well known, Gadamer introduces his understanding of play in the context of his reflections on the work of art. Yet the concept of play serves a much larger ontological role as a primary way of access to meaning.

In play, the distinction between player and game played is dimmed, as is the distinction between means and end. To play is to be set free from mere method and the mechanical pursuit of final goals.

If we examine how the word "play" is used and concentrate on its so-called transferred meanings we find talk of the play of light, the play of the waves, the play of a component in a bearing-case, the interplay of limbs, the play of forces, the play of gnats, even a play on words. In each case what is intended is the to-and-fro movement which is not tied to any goal which would bring it to an end. This accords with the original meaning of the word *spiel* as "dance," which is still found in many word forms. The movement which is play has no goal which brings it to an end; rather it renews itself in constant repetition. The movement backwards and forwards is obviously so central for the definition of a game that it is not important who or what performs this movement. The movement of play as such, has, as it were, no substrate.[20]

Play, as thus understood by Gadamer, is obviously more than the attitude of detached manipulation of possibilities. It functions to reveal the true nature of things by freeing us from the mechanical methods that promise premature closure. The to-and-fro movement of play enables us to enter fully into the radiant aspects of beings as these beings strive to become unhidden. To play, in this ontological sense, is to hover (note Karl Jaspers's understanding of *schwebend*) over diverse possibilities and perspectives. It is important to note that play is not substantive in the sense that some foundation underlies it. It exists simply as a movement of free interpretation.

In a passage remarkably akin to Royce, Gadamer states that play has a representative function beyond itself. The thing or rite being played points toward an audience.

All representation is potentially representative for someone. That this possibility is intended is the characteristic feature of the playful nature of art. The closed world of play lets down, as it were, one of its walls. A religious rite and a play in a theatre obviously do not represent in the same sense as the playing child. Their being is not exhausted by the fact that they represent; at the same time they point beyond themselves to the audience which is sharing in them.[21]

Representation can function in two modes; an object or event points to that of which it speaks (Peirce) and to an audience. The audience functions as the interpretee. Gadamer has rightly shown that play is not a solipsistic movement around purely private meanings. Rather, it enters into the communal structures and renders meaning available for further playful articulation. The audience becomes part of the play as it makes its to-and-fro movement between diverse meanings. The play and those played belong together in the playing. Hermeneutics is concerned with showing just what this to-and-fro movement has achieved.

---

[20]Gadamer, *Truth and Method*, 93.

[21]Ibid., 97.

Play, interpretive musement, and serial ramification all function to free interpretation from timeworn and mechanical paths. They cannot be reduced to methods if methods are understood as applying prefabricated means to envisioned ends. Peirce, Royce, and Gadamer all sought to free the interpretive process from the closure that kills meaning. In this sense they are in accord. Yet Gadamer errs in the direction of subjectivism. Even though he accounts for the reality of an audience, the interpretive process remains largely in the hands of the individual. This tendency toward subjectivism is reinforced by the above-mentioned "fusion of horizons." In the process of fusion, at least as rendered by Gadamer, the alien horizon (perspective) becomes so distorted as to become something else. The question is not whether changes occur—this much is granted by Royce—but rather, how we are to distinguish between severe distortion and interpretive enrichment. It is unclear how we could make such a distinction in practice, using Gadamer's hermeneutic principles.

Royce's community of interpretation functions to govern present and future interpretations so as to ensure that each sign manipulation is reasonably faithful to the previous signs and sign series. Each new interpretation must "listen" to the sign series that are handed to the interpreter by the community of interpretation. Royce's semiotic triad ensures that the manipulation of signs takes place in a controlled manner. It serves to reduce the danger of arbitrary interpretations. The community of interpretation is the horizon or perspective that governs sign articulation. It contains the necessary internal structure for providing objective understanding of signs.

Unlike the isolated individual, the community of interpretation is capable of sign articulation of a high degree of complexity. The community is spread across both time and individual interpreters. Past sign manipulations can be retained in communal memory, and present hermeneutic acts can be compared among individuals. No sign is condemned to purely private articulation. The community of interpretation is capable of detailed comparisons between interpretations. This comparative process ensures that a high degree of objectivity remains. Play itself, in the general sense, is governed by the community as it seeks to validate each interpretive addition to its hermeneutic stock.

Royce corrects a strong subjectivistic tendency in twentieth-century hermeneutic theory. His formulation, however, requires further articulation and reconstruction if it is to bear the burden of regrounding hermeneutics. In the next chapter I discuss the generic traits of what I shall call horizonal hermeneutics.

HORIZONAL HERMENEUTICS

Hermeneutics seeks to be horizonal in scope. It drives toward the encompassing perspective in which all signs are located vis-à-vis each other and in terms of the human communities that sustain and articulate them. Of course, such an encompassing view is unattainable within the relentless constraints of finitude. Yet it remains as the fundamental lure for our interpretive transactions. Furthermore, political and social distortions blunt the drive toward semiotic transparency and reduce the hermeneutic process to the mere validation of prior ideological structures. Finitude and ideology, the social expression of finitude, conspire to constrict the horizonal aspirations of hermeneutics. Horizonal hermeneutics attempts to reverse this process in terms of personal openness and communal democracy. The political dimension of interpretation should not be ignored in favor of a so-called neutral account of sign translation.

For Peirce and Royce, a horizonal hermeneutics could emerge only within the emancipatory structures of a certain kind of community life. Peirce argued that the community of science, using the methods of induction, deduction, and abduction, provided the most democratic structure for hermeneutics. Each scientist would suppress his or her ideological compulsions in order to become open to the convergent and time-bound consensus of the community of inquiry. In the indefinite future the community of science would arrive at the truth of its common body of signs and interpretations. For Royce, the Spirit-filled community of interpretation triumphs over finitude and political distortion whenever it allows the infinite interpreter to guide its internal hermeneutic acts. The marks of this Spirit can be seen whenever the interpretive process remains flexible and open to those enrichments of meaning that can come only from loyal interpreters who themselves stand under and within the loving pressures of the interpretive Spirit. Both Peirce and Royce struggled to find a way beyond the finite constraints of human interaction. Peirce posited the infinite long run as that which guaranteed the validation of interpretive acts. Royce posited the internal presence of the Spirit as that which validates each hermeneutic act. For both thinkers, the community functioned as the liberating horizon for interpretation.

Unfortunately, both Peirce and Royce confused descriptive with honorific traits in their delineation of the structure of communities. Peirce erred in making one kind of community normative for all kinds, while Royce ruled out in principle all of those communities that do not satisfy his stringent idealistic criteria. Not all communities need be scientific, nor need they be funded with the Spirit-Interpreter. Semiotic convergence and hermeneutic openness can prevail in a wide variety of communal structures and can often flower in contexts that Peirce and Royce would be forced to reject as inappropriate to the life of the interpreter.

We need here a more generic account of community and its bearing on the horizonal structures of interpretation. We must transcend the idealistic frameworks of Peirce and Royce, while serving their deeper impulses and insights. To do so entails an analysis of the notions of order, community, sign, and horizon. In the redefinition of these actualities, hermeneutics can find a categorial clearing that is adequate to its aspirations.

Hermeneutics is concerned with the general problem of place, namely, with locating each interpretation within its proper order or location. As such, hermeneutics is the self-conscious moment within topology. The finding of place (*topos*) is basic to the interpretive process. Each interpretation derives its meaning from the larger order that determines its scope and direction. The traditional discussion of the hermeneutic circle, particularly as found in Schleiermacher and Heidegger, expresses this fundamental insight that all interpretation is embedded in an order that encompasses the complex being interpreted. Whether the center or the circumference of this circle is being articulated, the ordinal nature of the act of interpretation is clear from the outset.

While it does not follow that every order is orderly, it does follow that every interpretation is order dependent. A sign, as the embodiment of an interpretation, points to its larger order as well as to innumerable subaltern orders within itself. Any given sign will illuminate an indefinite number of orders in an indefinite number of ways. The exploration of these structures is never a simple process, although rarely is some meaningful contour not found.

Minimally, an order is any grouping of traits in which the traits stand in some relation to each other. A given trait may be only weakly relevant to another within its order, but it will have a connection nonetheless.[1] Within the order of the complex of an automobile, for example, the color of the fabric on the seats will be only weakly relevant to the performance of the engine. The engine will function in specific ways, regardless of the

---

[1]For a detailed analysis of orders and of relevance, see Justus Buchler, *Metaphysics of Natural Complexes* (New York: Columbia University Press, 1966).

coloring of the seats. Yet the overall contour of the automobile—its complete meaning and scope within the life of its owner—will be determined by all of the traits that constitute it. While the upholstery color will not be directly relevant to the engine as engine, it will be indirectly relevant to it from the standpoint of the human purview that locates all traits within a larger sense of place. Bridges of meaning and relevance can be found that exhibit the ordinal placement of each trait.

While it is never possible to know all of the orders within which a sign belongs, it is possible to gain some sense of the various ordinal locations that govern a sign's life. A sign will be embedded in a variety of orders and exhibit a complex contour. However, the hermeneutic process need not attempt to pay heed to all of these orders in its drive toward the horizon. Some notion of selection must be operative if the human community is to achieve recognizable and specific meanings. At this stage it is important to note only that every interpretation takes place within an order that partially governs the intrinsic meaning of the sign being articulated. The sign itself contains its own subaltern orders and traits that need to be rendered intelligible to the community. All signs are thus order dependent and contain orders of lesser scope.

Every complex, whether it is a sign or not, is part of an order. Hence, to be is to be ordinally located and to contain subaltern orders. Signs are orders that have the added characteristic of meaning. A sign is a complex that means something to someone. Not all complexes are signs, although many are potential signs. It would grant too much metaphysical license to assert that all complexes are waiting to become signs, that is, to become meaningful to some interpreter. Some complexes are forever unknowable, while others are recalcitrant to meaning. A proper semiotic theory recognizes that nature contains innumerable complexes that cannot become signs. At the same time, however, it is equally clear that an indefinite number of complexes do become signs whenever they become available to human manipulation and analysis. There are no a priori boundaries determining some sort of set number to the list of possible and actual signs. The horizonal drive of the hermeneutic process precludes any predetermined number of signs.

The distinction between the complexes that are signs, whether actually or potentially, and those that are not, is crucial if the full integrity of signs is to be understood. Signs have to be separated from nonsigns so that the notion of meaning can become more sharply exhibited. When this distinction is made, semiotics can be properly located within a metaphysics of more general scope.

Whatever we can point to in any respect is thus an order and participates in other orders. At the same time, such an order will have innumerable subaltern orders that collectively determine part of its integrity.[2] As noted, some of these orders may be chaotic or lacking in formal structures, but they are orders nonetheless. Thus, for example, the history of quantum events in a given microsystem is disorderly, but these events remain as part of the order of that system and not another. Hermeneutics is thus order dependent. Any complex discriminated, insofar as it becomes or is a sign, is part of innumerable orders and contains its own orders. This realization forces us to broaden and radicalize the notion of the hermeneutic circle. Each sign is itself constituted by foreground and background and stands as a foreground for at least one other order. Horizonal hermeneutics is concerned with illuminating the sheer complexity of these interpretive circles.

While every complex is an order (and hence an order of orders), only some complexes are communities. It is crucial to exhibit the differentia of *communal* orders, but without intruding normative or honorific traits into the description. Such traits are relevant when dealing with types of community once we have isolated the minimal traits of any community per se.

Minimally, a community is constituted by two or more interpreters who have some signs in common. The initial issue concerns the traits of interpreters—namely, what makes a complex an interpreter and not merely a mind? At the very least, an interpreter must have a complex mental life—must entertain perceptions, conceptions, and have some openness to the traits of the world. Those complexes funded with mind stand in a unique relation to the orders of nature. They are constituted by numerous access structures that provide a conceptual and feeling-toned clearing on the world as a whole. These access structures are not merely mental constructs (although they are at least that) but represent the cumulative results of historical and personal encounters with complexes not of the self's own making. They frequently have a deep evolutionary foundation and have attested to their validity across time and space. The more powerful and generic access structures stem from the archetypes, which are located within the phylogenetic structures of the collective unconscious. The value of these access structures lies not only in their import for sheer survival and evolutionary competence but in their ability to open out traits and structures of nature as an indefinite "sphere" of orders. Hence, persons, as complexes funded with mind, are uniquely open to the world.

A collection of minds becomes a community whenever those minds have a number of important signs in common. Thus, for example, we have

---

[2]For Buchler, the integrity of a complex is its trait configuration within one specific order. The contour of a complex is the "sum" of its various integrities. The identity of a complex is the continuing relation between any given integrity and the contour—also known as the gross integrity.

a community whenever two or more persons are aware of the signs pertaining to a given sport. Insofar as the sport is meaningful to those persons, it stands as the common semiotic element in their convergent lives. Need these two or more persons be aware of each other in order for them to constitute a community? Most would argue that some form of communication must occur between them in order to warrant the claim that they constitute a specific community. It is not clear that this is a necessary trait for at least a minimal condition of community, because often a given individual will belong to many communities not within the purview of his or her awareness. Often, a specific event will strikingly illuminate a communal dimension previously hidden to the person. For example, the assassination of a leader may show that one had an identity, perhaps unconscious, with a social group not previously thought of as being part of one's life or value structure. Hence, it follows that we need not be conscious of all of the members of our given community, nor need we be in dialogue with any of its members.

Of course, such a definition of community—namely, that which is constituted by two or more minds with some signs in common—hardly satisfies our deeper hermeneutic sense. We seek a richer understanding of community life that shows how these common signs can represent the various foci for intersubjective communication and semiotic convergence. We must go beyond the minimal conditions of community in order to explore the traits of communities that are interpretive through and through.

Minds become interpreters when they add the traits of self-reflection, temporality, and intersubjectivity. Of course, most persons will exhibit these traits with varying degrees of fullness. Yet the success of the hermeneutic enterprise depends upon the maximization of these dimensions of human existence.

In self-reflection, the person achieves more than an awareness of external signs. In the reflexive turn, the self becomes aware of itself as a sign series with neither beginning nor end. The emergence of self-consciousness is coincident with the realization that no substantive or atemporal structure supports the identity of self. Rather, the self emerges as innumerable signs, each illuminating an aspect or dimension of the rich contour of personal identity. As Peirce argued, such a semiotic self has a fairly stable contour, but it does not have a static and hermeneutically neutral core that would be somehow intuited through our interpretive acts. The reflexive turn inaugurates the discovery that the self is constituted by innumerable sign series that serve to generate some form of self-identity through time. Insofar as these various series have some meaningful convergence, the self remains free from internal bifurcation and possible madness. Insofar as these series go their separate ways, the self may split apart into numerous part-selves with little or no common convergence.

As Peirce argued, some form of self-control is necessary if the self is to hold these signs in some meaningful contour.

To interpret is to gauge the meaning of a sign across time and space. No sign can be understood in an atemporal manner. Past dimensions of the sign must be compared with present dimensions so as to provide a consistent value for projected future meanings. Any given interpretation of a sign will change its meaning either by adding some new structure to the past accumulated values or by reconstructing inherited meanings. In the tactic of deconstruction, hidden or inverse meanings are evoked that alter the sign in dramatic ways. Together these methods or tactics enrich and transform sign meaning through time. A sign interpreted is a sign changed. Consider the complex sign (or sign series) of a text such as the Bible. A deconstructive reading would isolate and invert the masculine and logocentric traits of the divine nature, particularly as presented in the so-called Old Testament. The sign values inherited by the community of biblical interpretation would receive a decisive inversion into something sinister and alien. A certain continuity would be evident, however, in that a specific body of signs would remain dominant for a body of interpreters. It is not that we have totally new signs but that inherited signs receive striking new values. In colloquial terms we can be driven to ask, "Which Bible are they reading anyway?" The answer is that they are reading the same body of signs available to us. The deconstruction of a meaning is as much an enrichment as the mere augmentation of a commonly accepted interpretation. These processes are fully temporal in that they entail some notion of a hoped-for convergence in the ideal or proximate future. Past and present sign meanings serve a future goal that may or may not be conscious or articulated.

As noted in the previous chapter, Gadamer considers this internal temporality fundamental to the notion of horizon. Whenever an interpreter assimilates and manipulates sign material, the three modes of temporality are automatically brought into play. Insofar as a sign is order dependent, it must contain innumerable ramifications that hark back to a dimly felt past that may eclipse the life span of a given interpreter. By the same token, the sign must contain leadings that point ineluctably toward some forms of convergence in the near or remote future. That the present bristles with past and future radii is one of the givens of the interpretive life.

Temporality and self-reflection are necessary constituents in the highly differentiated phenomenon of intersubjectivity. As Royce argued, self-consciousness emerges out of social and temporal contrast with other selves. It is impossible to separate the self from the communities within which it is embedded. To have a personal contour is to have emerged from communal transactions of greater and lesser scope. The sheer difference between the I and the not-I, a difference with highly shifting boundaries, emerges from intersubjective contrasts.

It is important that we do not hypostatize intersubjectivity into some kind of species being or universal essence. Such an ontological analysis of human community betrays an inability to understand the indefinite complexity of communication and the evolution of shared meanings. A community is no more an essence of intersubjective consciousness (Husserl) than it is an eternal form that prescinds from the ravages of disloyalty and betrayal. At the other extreme, we must reject the perspective of social atomism, which would deny that intersubjectivity has traits not found in the sheer enumeration of finite selves. A living interpretive community is one that emerges from natural enabling conditions that may support one type of community but not another and may ensure the demise of the very community that emerged in the first place. The finite interpreter is not somehow added to an already preconstituted community as one more member but derives his or her very meaning only through those intersubjective transactions that enrich the scope and contour of the community.

A mind thus becomes an interpreter whenever the traits of self-reflection, temporality, and intersubjectivity function together to secure the ongoing hermeneutic process. All three traits, taken separately or in consort, are intrinsically communal. Self-reflection reveals an intrasubjective community of innumerable signs and sign series that together serve to secure self-identity through time. Temporality, insofar as it provides access structures to nature, opens out into the communal dimension of signs. Any given sign will carry the weight of human community in its prior and hoped-for interpretive bounty. Varying degrees of semiotic density will be manifest in signs and their attendant series. The past and future will be part of the ordinal and communal dimension of signs. Finally, intersubjectivity is most obviously communal in that the traits of contrast and convergence between interpreters emerge as the most fundamental. Any given interpreter will thus exhibit communal structures in all of these dimensions of the human process.

We have considered signs and sign series in analyzing orders and communities. We are now ready to investigate the specific traits of signs as they pertain to the life of interpretation. I articulate here six aspects of the life of signs, which can be understood to represent degrees of scope, moving from the least generic toward the most generic. On the highest level, signs refer to that which is neither another sign nor a trait within nature or the world.

Crucial to all six dimensions of sign functions is the notion of reference or relation. Reference is one type of relation and entails that the sign points to something in an asymmetrical manner. The sign points to a local (subaltern) or regional trait, but that trait need not point back to the sign. A stop sign, for example, functioning in what Peirce would call an indexical fashion, points to a specific state of affairs involving a road intersection. As such, the sign points to something that has regional and general traits. But the road configuration does not point back to the sign and enhance its meaning. Said differently, the sign derives its meaning as a pointing index from the road configuration that brought it into being, but the road configuration need not, in order to prevail, have a stop sign as part of its contour. Within the order of human convention, of course, a stop sign may be likely, but it is not a necessary component in the order of particular road configurations. The sign is thus dependent on the road, whereas the road is not dependent on the sign. This correlation of dependence and independence is one form of asymmetrical relation. Other forms involve temporal or differently defined spatial relations.

If sign references are asymmetrical, sign relations are symmetrical but in differing ways. A sign and its correlate are symmetrical in that they are mutually implicated in determining each other's contour. Each relation enhances and transforms the relata and generates novel, if ofttimes trivial, additions to the semiotic stock. Thus, for example, a sign relates to a given interpreter in a symmetrical manner. The interpreter assimilates pregiven meanings in the sign and works to alter and deepen those meanings. These additions subsequently form part of the evolving contour of the sign. This process is dialectic in that both relata are transformed in the process of interpretation. As noted above, a sign interpreted is a sign changed. Such a process must be symmetrical and temporal.

Now that we have seen the broad distinction between asymmetrical reference and symmetrical relation, we must consider all of the dimensions of sign functioning. Two of those dimensions involve asymmetrical reference relations, while four involve symmetrical relations proper. Any given sign will participate in most of these dimensions but with differing degrees of instantiation. The fullest signs will participate in all six dimensions. To isolate any one dimension is to do violence to the richness of sign function. Yet this process of prescinding is essential if the sheer complexity of sign systems is to be laid bare.

On the first and least generic level is the reference of the sign to a local or subaltern trait. Such a trait is one of limited scope and import and represents a minor constituent in a complex. For example, the prevalence of the color red in a painting by Cézanne may function in a limited way to enhance the three more basic color groups of blue, green, and brown. Not only is it a local trait within the complex of the painting, but it serves as a sign insofar as it refers to either a trait in nature or a trait within the world of the work of art itself. It points to regional traits of larger scope and helps to enrich their contour. Of course, the relation between local and regional traits need not be spatial. The prevalence of a specific tone in a piece of music may serve to reinforce regional motifs, while retaining its own independence.

Insofar as a complex sign refers to a local trait in one of its dimensions, it carries minimal semiotic density. One way of understanding the difference between a local and regional trait, in addition to referring to degrees of scope, is in terms of the depth of meaning conveyed. Local traits are, by definition, unable to sustain meaning beyond a certain minimal context. Returning to our example of a painting by Cézanne, the local color traits, while enhancing the value of the larger color fields, fail on their own to sustain extensive aesthetic value. If they were to be isolated from the regional traits that they serve, they would soon reveal their lack of semiotic density.

Regional traits are more than the mere sum of local traits but represent fairly autonomous and distinct values. As such they order and govern the local traits that fall within their purview. The movement from local to regional structures often entails a conceptual or experiential leap from one dimension of complexity to another. One cannot enumerate the sum of local traits and thereby gain access to the regional configurations within a specific complex. Since regional traits represent a higher level of governance and exhibit greater degrees of semiotic density and scope than the "totality" of local traits, it follows that they can be arrived at only by shifting to a different axis of apprehension. This new axis reveals the ontological difference between local and regional structures. The more complex the phenomenon being articulated, the more dramatic and novel the divide between local and regional structures.

Signs functioning on the second level refer to regional structures and are asymmetrical but embody the greater scope and density of their referent and hence are of more import for the human process than signs that refer to local traits. The implied hierarchy between local and regional traits is not a hierarchy of being. Regional traits are not more real than local traits, whatever one could mean by "more real," but represent an increment in richness and inclusiveness. Such signs are more generic and serve to bring more of the world into unhiddenness than do signs with local referents.

Is the difference between the local and regional conventional or natural? Do the orders of nature suggest this difference, or is it merely a function of human selection? The answer is not always simple. In many cases—for example, those pertaining to selective processes of inquiry in the sciences—regional traits emerge with a fair degree of regularity and compulsion, leading one to the assumption that nature somehow manifests this distinction to human probing. That all organisms exhibit the twin dimensions of vulnerability to natural selection and the internal pressures of random variation indicates that these traits are regional and not merely local. They are pervasive and fundamental. At the other extreme, the selection of nonlocal traits in ordinary conversation is often fraught with difficulty. Just which phrases or utterances are revelatory of the basic contour of the self and which are not? For a practicing psychologist, for example, this question can assume primary import especially because of its recalcitrance. Armed with the archetype theory, such a psychological query can begin to sift out local from regional structures and can thus prepare the way for appropriate arts of healing.

Whether the distinction between local and regional traits is merely conventional or is governed by highly compulsive natural structures, the difference for sign theory is clear. Insofar as a sign contains enhanced scope and density, it is more likely to embody a regional trait. As such it carries a greater interpretive burden than its local cousins and functions more fully within the life of the finite interpreter and the various communities within which such an interpreter is embedded. Local traits are placed and ordered by regional traits, although some local traits may have only a minimal relation to their more generic relatives. Within works of art one of the criteria for greatness would be the success with which regional and local traits amplify each other, ensuring both complexity and configurational integrity.

Signs, insofar as they function to refer to local or regional traits, are internally triadic. For Royce, the triadicity on this level is manifest in the contrast between percept, concept, and interpretation. The sign, as the embodiment of the interpretation, holds percept and concept together in their third value, which is the specific interpretation. This internal triad is, as noted previously, the hermeneutic triad. On the next generic level, the third level of sign function, the semiotic triad emerges. This level or dimension is the relation, fully symmetrical, between a sign and its interpreter. Of course, this dimension is never absent, and we isolate it as a stage only through a process of prescinding.

The interpreter assimilates and manipulates the sign in order to articulate and deepen its meaning. Signs are not discrete meaning-packets that somehow only need to be pried open in order to reveal their bounty. A better analogy is that of the arena, which is open for a variety of onstage performances and actions. Meanings may wait in the wings as specific dramas unfold. Each scene may reveal different leadings or different plot lines. A sign is thus an interpretive clearing with permeable boundaries, always ready for yet one more stage appearance or cameo role. Signs are open on all sides, both temporally and relationally. Any time a sign has an impact on the human process it enriches its contour and broadens its scope and density.

The semiotic triad is between a given sign, its interpreter, and the implied interpretee for whom the sign is articulated. The interpretee is merely implied on this level and fully emerges only on the fourth level of sign function. Of course, the interpreter, using reflexive communication, can function as both interpreter and interpretee. Insofar as the self is constituted by innumerable sign series and part-selves, it can be both the person interpreting and the person for whom the interpretation is made. Of course, such an internal communal transaction is possible only because of the pervasive presence of intersubjectivity, which provides the primary access structures for intrasubjectivity. As Royce argued, social contrast is the enabling condition for internal dialogue.

On the fourth level of sign function, the interpretee emerges in an explicit manner. A given interpreter hands his or her interpretation, embodied in a sign, to another in order to test and validate a given understanding. The sign becomes further ramified and articulated by the interpretee, who in turn either hands it back to the original interpreter or passes it on to another interpretee. The initial semiotic triad explodes into innumerable triads as sign interpretation becomes more fully communal. The triads link up to generate a series of structures that branch out in an indefinite number of directions. The relation between the sign, the interpreter, and the interpretee secures genuine community. As noted, insofar as two or more interpreters have one dominant sign in common, they constitute a community in the minimal sense. Only on the fourth level of sign function can we speak properly of human community. Of course, a community of interpretation will have additional traits besides those minimal ones just indicated. I will describe such traits shortly.

We must not unduly mix metaphors. Whenever a sign is handed to another person, it retains its open-ended character, even though it retains just the features that it has in its transmission. What is passed on is not a carefully bounded container of meaning but an arena of meanings waiting for further plot development. The image is not so much that of passing the baton in a race as that of handing the stage over to other actors with specific, if flexible, roles to play. Semiotic boundaries may expand or contract, but they rarely remain static. The wealth of a community is best measured by its ability to sustain semiotic expansion against the twin powers of habit and inertia.

Such communal transmission is fraught with difficulty. Prior ideological and horizonal commitments, whether consciously defended or blindly endured, blunt the open movement of sign articulation. In order to ensure that sign translation is free and judicious on this fourth level—the level pertaining to signs, interpreters, and interpretees—it is necessary to argue for certain normative aspects of communal life. It is not sufficient merely to state the bare minimal conditions of communal existence. Beyond the requirement that two or more interpreters have a dominant sign in common must be the deeper structural values that secure a democracy of sign transmission. Not all communities are genuine communities of interpretation or, better, communities of articulation. Before proceeding to an analysis of the fifth and sixth dimensions of sign function, we must examine the traits of a fully democratic interpretive community.

A hermeneutic community, otherwise described as a community of articulation or interpretation, can emerge only when interpreters have the necessary freedom to give novel and enriched meanings to the common body of signs. Of course, any given interpreter will be the locus where innumerable communities intersect. This complex intersection entails a minimal level of self-control if bifurcation is to be avoided. Within the individual these pressures can become acute. The hermeneutic community must honor these tensions and provide an adequate order within which they can find some kind of stable contour. Hence the true interpretive community must both allow personal freedom and help to secure intra-subjective harmony. This harmony, of course, need not entail empty uniformity. In granting the individual the appropriate maneuvering room, the community must also provide meaningful boundaries for imaginative reach.

Individual liberty does not constitute a sufficient condition for the hermeneutic community. Some form of conscious convergence must also prevail as the locus of future aspiration for the members of the social order. A democracy is not merely the sum total of liberated individuals but requires institutional and social convergence around shared values and goals. Without this common future the sign process would degenerate into a pluralistic cacophony of discordant and competing sounds.

Individual freedom and social convergence reinforce each other whenever the sign process is open-ended and driven toward generic encompassment. The past semiotic wealth of the community is not the seedbed for endless recollection but stands as the originating ground for novel delineations. Origin and expectation stand as the two poles for communal transaction. Insofar as the signs of origin, whether mythical or not, stand under the liberating power of the eschatological, they serve to open out the individual to that which transcends the habitual and the ideological. The semiotic triad remains fluid and expanding under the impress of positive expectation. Convergence does not negate origin or the individual but locates both under the lure that quickens the community toward justice.

For Royce, loyalty to loyalty functions as the highest human act of will in the hermeneutic community. Within the spirit of loyalty the finite interpreter feels the pull of other genuine loyalties and struggles toward the meaningful convergence that represents the deepest aspiration of the social order. A loyal interpreter will let no true loyalty die. Any sign series emergent from such a loyalty must become part of the general semiotic life of the community. Its contributions will become part of the evolving wealth of all interpreters. Disloyal deeds, embodied in active sign systems, will receive their proper criticism and condemnation from the loyal interpreters who constitute the true core of the hermeneutic community. The concept of loyalty to loyalty is not a mere tautology but ensures that no other loyalty be allowed that destroys the very spirit of loyalty. Loyalty to a band of robbers is not genuine loyalty because such loyalty, by definition, insists on shattering the loyalties of some other groups. Loyalty to a heteronomous political faction is not genuine loyalty because it destroys the very possibility of a liberated community. The only specific loyalty allowed is that which serves to open up semiotic possibilities for others. Within the concept of loyalty is an implied commitment to the Kantian Kingdom of Ends, which demands that no individual be treated as a means merely but as someone of unconditional worth. The herme-neutic community ensures the worth of all interpreters, whether or not they are loyal. Disloyal interpreters are corrected by the community whenever they threaten to destroy genuine convergence and personal freedom.

The hermeneutic community may of course represent a small minor-ity within the empirical community under consideration. The creative minority may be the internal teleological core of the larger community and represent its hope for radical self-transcendence. Sheer size and heter-onomous power frequently render the hermeneutic community impo-tent. The failure of such communities gives no ground for triumphal claims. One can argue that the tragic denial of such fragmented com-munities of interpretation is the fundamental lesson of history. Royce's celebration of the grace-filled Beloved Community should not blind us to the fact that such communities rarely free themselves from the heteron-omous structures that surround them. That they do so at all is a testa-ment to the power of hermeneutic expansion and semiotic enrichment.

The emergence of the genuine interpretive community is a moment within the self-transcendence of humanity. It is appropriate to celebrate this triumph against inertia and heteronomous distortion. More impor-tant, it is necessary to recognize that such a flowering is the result of a form of grace that transforms the interpretive life of individuals. If we can speak of a hermeneutic grace, it follows that it is most fully manifest in communities that become momentarily freed from the fragmentary real-ity of history.

The sign process embodies the life of the communities that sustain it. This life emerges more fully when a fifth dimension of sign function is exhibited. While the fourth dimension deals with the correlation between sign, interpreter, and interpretee, the fifth deals with the unfolding of signs in indefinitely extended triads. This dimension is, of course, hid-den within the fourth and represents its fulfillment through time and space. Signs link together to form discrete series with their own lines of convergence and their own contours. We call this process serial ramifi-cation. Insofar as a sign prevails, it will be part of at least one sign series, however minimal the scope of that series. Such series govern and order the life histories of the signs functioning within them. At the same time, a given sign may exert a counterpressure on its specific series and force the other signs to alter their integrity and meaning. This relation is fully symmetrical, as both relata may be transformed in the relation.

Sign series may prevail within reflexive (intrasubjective) community or within the life of the community of interpretation. The boundaries be-tween internal and external series are hard to draw, as internal series de-rive their meaning from external meaning structures. Within human cultural evolution these boundaries have constantly been redefined. The psychoanalytic theory of projection has forced us to recognize that many so-called external sign series are actually internal series that are driven toward outward expression as a means of avoiding realizations that might disturb the general psychic economy. The withdrawal of such projections is the fundamental motor force for social and cultural evolution. Yet even within the relentless and corrosive skepticism of modernity, such an inversion of internal and external series is fraught with difficulty. It is a basic truth that no absolute and atemporal circle can be drawn that would eliminate the struggle against projections.

The constituents within a sign series are related to each other in some respect. However, weak and strong forms of relevance are possible. For example, the formal language changes involved in a biblical text such as the Book of Job may be strongly relevant to the overall meaning of the text. One author may view the problem of unwarranted suffering differently from another. Because of this shift, the signs in one part of the book may strikingly illuminate the signs in the other. On the other hand, the specific expressions within the lament of Job may have only a weak bearing on the speeches offered by his friends. On an even weaker level of relevance, the number of Job's friends may have only a minimal bearing on the overall contour of the book. Any sign in a sign series will have varying degrees of relevance to other signs. The same sign may be strongly relevant to another sign or part-series, while being weakly relevant to another.

No sign series will prevail in total isolation from other series. At some point it must intersect with at least one other series. Serial ramification is in principle without a predetermined circumference. Of course, part of a given series may intersect with one series, while another part of that same series may intersect with another but not the first. This process may become indefinitely complex. The hermeneutic process must attempt to delineate all of these branchings yet will ultimately fail to flesh out the full contour of any series and its intersections. The image is that of a forest of trees with interlocking yet hidden roots. Does this sheer multiplicity of meanings render hermeneutics powerless? Not unless complete atemporal comprehension is sought. The community of interpretation will make the necessary choices concerning which sign series are more important for a selective process of query and which series serve in an auxiliary role. These decisions are subject to correction as new signs and their interpreted meanings invert the value hierarchies of the community. Nature and history combine to govern the selection process so that not all signs are of equal weight or import. Critical common sense and refined query conspire to move interpretation in positive directions.

Each sign series has its own natural history. While no series will have an absolute beginning or first sign, it will have a penumbra of origin, whether from another series or through a creative irruption that gives birth to a unique sign cluster. By the same token, no sign series will have an absolute end. Even the death of a human individual and his or her reflexive community will leave some traces, however short-lived or weak.

While a given series may eventually cease to prevail as a specific integrity, ramificational possibilities will always prevail or be available whenever there are interpreters. Serial ramification encompasses the number of attained ramifications and stands as a lure for further sign unfolding.

Sign series are rarely "satisfied" with their specific scope at a given time. Something akin to a generic hunger animates each series as it drives toward the Encompassing itself. No series will reach totality, yet no series will be completely free from the longing for full encompassment. Each series will struggle to bring more and more of nature within its purview. Each series, dependent for its existence upon one or more interpreters, will both overreach its boundaries and misrepresent other series. For example, the psychosexual model of Freudian analysis represents a sign series that attempts to encompass all of personal and collective human reality within one categorical array that claims sufficiency and completeness. At the same time, the psychoanalytic framework represents other alternative sign series as mere subaltern components within its larger horizon. These subaltern series may be augmentations or distortions, but they are denied their own autonomy. Not all sign series so fully embody this imperial intent, yet it slumbers within each of them insofar as they function at all. Severe mental illness can be defined as the result of a hubristic and private sign series that cannot admit the reality of other, competing series.

Two ways show themselves as limiting the scope of serial ramification without withering the healthy growth that is necessary to sign systems. The first is that of proper serial intersection, in which one series becomes open to the pressures of another such that its own scope is both limited and, in a very different way, enhanced. The series is limited insofar as it becomes a subaltern series within another. Or, less violently, it becomes coequal to another series with similar scope and focus. The series is enhanced insofar as it enriches its semiotic stock by the addition of meanings outside its original perspective or perspectives. Its "internal" integrity may be altered, whether through a straightforward augmentation or through a novel coalescence. Serial ramification must strive toward expansion and intersection so that the twin demands of encompassment and limitation can be met. This process is fundamental to the health of the community of interpreters, who must honor more sign series than they know and must sustain more intersections than they can control.

Of the two forms of limitation, serial intersection and the movement toward the Encompassing, the latter is rarer and more important to the life of the community. Serial intersection remains on the fifth level of sign function insofar as it is a moment within the self-transparency of serial ramification. The movement toward the Encompassing is the sixth and final dimension of sign function and brings the sign relation into the sphere of religion. On this sixth level a sign truly emerges as a symbol and becomes a clearing through which the Encompassing exerts its uncanny lure for human existence. We must distinguish between symbols of the Encompassing and all other signs if we are to gain a glimpse into that reality that itself is not another sign.

Above, we used the notion of semiotic density as a means of illuminating the generic scope of a sign. Insofar as a sign on the second level refers to a regional trait, it has more scope and density (meaning) than a sign referring to a local trait on the first level. As we move through the other dimensions of sign function, the scope of the sign increases to include interpreters on the third level and the larger community of interpreters and interpretees on the fourth level. On the fifth level, the sign is related to innumerable sign series that branch out in all directions. Any sign that is part of the process of serial ramification will have a very high degree of density. This density of meaning may dwarf the powers of the finite interpreter. It may even lie beyond the interpretive reach of the hermeneutic community. Part of this density must often be ignored by given interpreters in order to facilitate the concrete tasks of communication. The more dimensions exhibited by a sign, the more semiotic load carried. Of course, each sign participates in all six dimensions of sign function, but most do so in a weak or partial manner. Only rarely will a sign be rich enough to embody all six dimensions in such a way as to do full justice to all of the levels. The only signs that consistently do so are those of religion.

A religious symbol has a curious relation to the phenomenon of semiotic density. By definition, it must carry the density of meaning found on the first five levels. Hence it will refer to local and regional traits and be related to interpreters, interpretees, and other signs. For example, the symbol of the cross, perhaps the ultimate symbol for human religious apprehension, will embody the local traits of its medium of expression, whether of wood or other material. At the same time, the specific configuration of the cross—for example, Byzantine, Canterbury, or Maltese—will exhibit regional traits that can often be identified with a particular region and/or period. These regional configurations are of greater hermeneutic import than the local traits of the material used. Of course, whenever an exotic material is used in the manufacture of a cross, it can function as a regional trait.

On the next level, the cross is related to a specific interpreter who attempts to understand its import for human existence. On the fourth level, the cross deepens its meaning whenever it becomes the dominant object of a community of interpretation that struggles to flesh out its value. Because of the unusual nature of this particular symbol, the community of interpretation connected with it has great scope and depth. It reaches back across numerous centuries and cultures with a vast diversity of sign series. Again, by definition, such a community participates in sign series with neither fixed beginning nor predictable end. Of all symbols, the cross seems to carry the greatest density of meaning for interpreters within the Western traditions.

Yet we cannot remain on this level if the sign of the cross is to be a true symbol. Other signs participate on all five levels of sign function with at least analogous power and scope. The differentiation between a sign, however rich in import for the human process, and a genuine symbol lies in the inversion of meaning that occurs on the sixth level. For it is on this level that the sign breaks free from itself in order to become transparent to something radically other.

A sign becomes a symbol when it becomes open to the Encompassing measure that itself is not a sign or symbol. At this point the sign undergoes a radical transformation in which its density is sacrificed for something else. The plenitude of meaning, always crowding around the sign in its various functions, gives way to an emptiness that momentarily pushes the semiotic import aside. The sign, qua symbol, achieves a radiant emptiness that lets all finite meanings drop away so that the light of the Encompassing may emerge in its purity. The specific meanings embedded in the sign in its other dimensions of sign function wait in the wings, as it were, to return once the power of the Encompassing recedes from view.

Returning to the symbol of the cross, we can see how this process emerges. The cross carries a tremendous semiotic load as a sign of the divine/human drama of redemption. It has cultural, historical, psychological, theological, and aesthetic values that can be articulated and ramified by the community of interpretation. This semiotic amplification represents one of the fundamental threads running throughout Western civilization. Yet this semiotic wealth is not the true meaning of this symbol. The cross is perhaps unique among dominant symbols in that it has the power to negate itself from within. The symbol of crucifixion specifically denies that any human or communal value can be attached to this reality. The cross curiously inverts itself whenever we try to fill it with further human content. In its self-negation, the cross breaks open to that which vastly outstrips human categorical projections.

The Encompassing is that reality that is revealed through genuine religious symbols. Whether or not the cross is the most radical symbol of the Encompassing, it fulfills its role whenever emptiness takes the place of semiotic density. This emptiness is not a nihilistic absence of meaning but a radiant evocation of a different kind of meaning not circumscribed by the signs of the community and its interpreters. The symbol momentarily places its other sign functions in eclipse so that the deeper reality of the Encompassing may be sensed.

Whenever a sign leaps into the final level of sign function, it becomes altered on its other levels as well. Once a sign has broken itself on the Encompassing, its references and relations become transformed and filled with an ultimate import that eludes easy capture. Local and regional traits take on a special transparency that points to something not part of the cluster of traits. Interpreters become arrested in their semiotic flights and are forced to encounter something that resists all of their projective as-pirations. The community itself is lured by something that lies beyond the scope of every perspective and horizon. This lure, elusive in its presence, stands as the moment of radical grace within the fitful life of the body of interpreters.

How does the Encompassing, manifest in the lure that speaks through religious symbols, differ from the horizons or perspectives that govern personal and communal life? We must clarify this issue before we can gain adequate insight into the sixth dimension of sign function.

Whatever is, is an order and, by implication, an order of orders. Orders that are humanly occupied are perspectives or horizons that add the traits of awareness, expandability, and, more rarely, self-conscious trans-formation. A horizon is a categorical and experiential clearing that locates the human process within a sphere of openness. All persons occupy ho-rizons, regardless of the necessary ignorance of the scope and integrity of the horizon itself. A horizon rarely becomes the object of self-con-scious probing and articulation. Yet the shocks and breaks of personal and communal life serve to make horizons more fully self-transparent. Pre-human forms may have horizons in some minimal sense, and this aware-ness should govern any general hermeneutics of nature. It is important to stress that a horizon is not merely a subjective projection but somehow stands between person and world as a third actuality, keeping each open to the other. The realm of the horizon is perhaps best characterized by the metaphor of the Midworld.[3] The Midworld stands between subject and object and is constituted by signs and interpretations that represent the truths of the community.

Horizons have a hunger for generic expansion and encompassment. Within the internal structure of any given horizon is the desire to become identical to the world itself and, in doing so, to forget the distance sepa-rating a human perspective from the domain of natural complexes that the perspective attempts to exhibit. It is part of the very logic of a horizon that it forgets that it is a horizon. This forgetfulness can be overcome not from within the horizon itself but only through its self-humiliation in the face of that which is never a horizon or even a horizon of horizons. A striking dialectic prevails between horizonal triumphalism and the rarer and more profound moments in which the horizon embraces its own cross, which, curiously, brings it into its own for the first time. The hori-

---

[3]The philosopher John William Miller has explored the perspectival dimen-sions of what he calls the Midworld in a number of works. Of particular impor-tance is *The Midworld of Symbols and Functioning Objects* (New York: Norton, 1982). For an analysis of this notion, see my "John William Miller and the Ontology of the Midworld," *Transactions of the Charles S. Peirce Society* 22:2 (Spring 1986): 165-88.

zon is broken open by the plenitude of the Midworld and, more radically, by the Encompassing.

A horizon is thus a humanly occupied order, located in the Midworld, which stands as a third actuality uniting persons and nature. It is both subjective and objective in different respects and in varying degrees. Insofar as a horizon is not open to communal intersection and transformation, it remains more subjective than objective. Whenever the horizon becomes sensitive to the shocks of nature (Peirce's seconds) and to the richness and integrity of other horizons, it moves toward the objective. Horizons differ in scope and complexity. The Midworld is the generic actuality that "contains" all of the horizons sustained by the human process. Cultural evolution can be defined as the historical expansion of the Midworld as it adds more signs to its constitution.

The Midworld, as the "sum" of all horizons, encompasses all given horizons. At the same time, it stands as the domain within which horizons may intersect and become transparent to each other. The Midworld reaches down into both nature and human community to ensure that the semiotic process remains embedded in realities that are not signs. While the Midworld contains many kingdoms, it retains sufficient stability to support human meanings. In a very real sense, the Midworld is that which enables persons to have and enjoy horizons at all.

The "sum" of all actual and possible horizons cannot constitute the Encompassing itself. Nor can the Midworld, as the location for all horizons, whether human or animal, function as the Encompassing. This ultimate reality cannot function as the positive location or order for anything else. It is neither a sign nor a horizon but stands as that which is radically other to all horizonal realities. It is not discoverable through specific semiotic structures or through the use of analogy. The only access we have to the Encompassing is through a kind of *via negativa* that shatters all categorial projections.[4]

Beyond the Midworld lies that which encompasses all complexes and signs. The Encompassing is without a positive contour that could somehow become available to human query. It negates all attempts to probe its nature, even while announcing itself at the edges of all horizons. In its curious dialectic of presence and absence, it both hides and shows itself to the finite interpreter. It is never come upon directly but must be caught out of the corner of the hermeneutic eye. While we cannot appropriate the Encompassing through the "analogy of being," we can use analogy

---

[4]The pioneering work on the concept of the Encompassing (*das Umgreifende*) was done by Karl Jaspers. Of particular importance is his work *Von der Wahrheit*, large sections of which have recently been translated and appear in *Karl Jaspers: Basic Philosophical Writings*, ed. and trans. Edith Ehrlich, Leonard H. Ehrlich, and George B. Pepper (Athens: Ohio University Press, 1986).

to give us some rudimentary indications as to its nature, remembering that all analogies fail when pushed toward the Encompassing itself.

No horizon is ever fully self-transparent to the person who occupies it or, better, is occupied by it. It retains traits that may forever be hidden to its "owner" and to those who attempt to explore it from outside. The horizon is vastly larger in scope than those dimensions of it that are known or even knowable. Frequently, some of these hidden traits emerge into consciousness whenever the horizon collides with an alien horizon that forces it to become more fully transparent to itself. Each horizon contains ideological structures that are rarely, if ever, made the object of thematic and critical awareness. Part of the perennial tragedy of communal life is this ultimate recalcitrance on the part of horizons to reveal all of their idiosyncratic and demonic traits. Since the horizon is always more than can ever be known about it, it functions, by analogy, as an encompassing order that forever recedes from view. The analogy breaks down, however, when it is recognized that the hidden dimension of the horizon still contains positive traits that belong to a finite and time-bound perspective. One horizon will still differ from another and retain just the traits that it has, no matter how deeply submerged they may be from the standpoint of the sign community.

The Encompassing remains hidden, but it never hides specific and perspectival traits that could somehow reveal themselves in time. The only positive trait of the Encompassing itself is its relation to that which is encompassed. It stands as the measure for signs, horizons, and the Midworld but itself is never measured or encompassed. It lures all symbols (signs with religious import) into a form of self-denial such that the density of sign meaning gives way to the emptiness within which the ultimate import of the Encompassing shows itself. While persons are encompassed by nature and interpretive communities, all finite realities receive their measure from that which forever lies beyond the scope of our horizons.

The metaphor of the lure best captures the relational dimension of the Encompassing. This lure functions in two ways, one of them leading directly to the other through a logic that is as relentless as it is liberating. On the first level, the lure of the Encompassing is manifest in the crucifixion (what Jaspers calls *scheitern*), which breaks the power of the horizon and its attendant sign series. From the standpoint of religion this moment is the encounter with the wrath of God. As Luther persuasively argued, this wrath is merely the prelude to the deeper and more pervasive love of God, which locates and transforms the wrath that brings horizonal triumphalism to an end.[5] Beyond self-glorification lies the second

---

[5]I refer, of course, to Luther's fundamental and still relevant distinction between the theology of glory and the theology of the cross. Hermeneutics must appropriate this distinction if it is to experience its own shattering in the power of the Encompassing.

dimension of the lure of the Encompassing, which is manifest as the radical openness to that which has no contour. In religious language, this is the moment of resurrection, in which the limitations painfully manifest in horizonal crucifixion are overcome as the horizon learns a sense of its own finitude, while experiencing the possibility of that which has no limitations.

The lure coaxes horizons toward their own limits and enables them to endure the shipwreck that awaits them. Within its inner logic it moves beyond shipwreck toward the ever-receding power that keeps the world open. The opening power of the Encompassing works quietly against those forms of demonic closure that punctuate human and natural history. The absolute abyss between the finite and that which is not finite is held open by the love of the Encompassing for that which is encompassed.[6] This love is most dramatically manifest from within the heart of the wrath that breaks all horizons. Love always overcomes the wrath that is its necessary circumference.

The fulfillment of horizonal hermeneutics is found in the transforming agapistic love that fills the community with the hope of redemption. Each act of interpretation, no matter how casual or trivial, receives its measure from the eschatological power of liberating love. This is the animating core of genuine community and the hope of all interpretation. Without this hope we would be bereft of the Encompassing measure that is the origin and goal of all life.

---

[6]This distinction between the finite and the nonfinite represents a conceptual redefinition of what Heidegger has called the "ontological difference." For a more detailed treatment of this theme, see my "Naturalism, Measure, and the Ontological Difference," *Southern Journal of Philosophy* 23:1 (Spring 1985): 19-32.

ROYCE ON PAUL
AND THE PRIMITIVE CHURCH

In exhibiting the traits of the community of interpretation, Royce had a paradigm community in mind in the primitive church of early Christianity. The physical and theological journeys of Paul form the inner thread of these fragile communities, and Royce takes pains to show that Paul was able to work through the sayings of Jesus in such a way as to find a theology adequate to the living church. This theology focused on the church as the body of Christ, which was the real locus of the divine drama in history after the events of the Crucifixion and Resurrection had taken place. Outside of this community, which was grounded in the Spirit of loyalty, Christ was without voice or form. Within the community, the Spirit could quicken the lives of believers in anticipation of the eschatological drama that would transform the structures of history.

In the Pauline Epistles, the fragmentary sayings of Jesus assume the shape and emphasis that became normative for the evolving church. Paul ignored the biographical and historical aspects of the founder in order to stress the centrality of his eschatological vision for a transformed humanity in time. For Royce, Paul was among the first of Western thinkers to probe into the dynamic structures of community and to show how these structures are animated and deepened by the presence of the Holy Spirit as the agency of Christ through time. Paul's vision of love, as the divine/human expression of loyalty, became the ethical core for his understanding of the community as the body of Christ. In a very real sense, Pauline Christology is a dimension of the metaphysics of community and functioned to give substance to the self-consciousness of the emerging primitive communities of faith. The loyalty embodied in the life and death of Jesus was the paradigm for the loyalty that cemented the primitive church against internal and external bifurcation and dissolution. Within the pressures of the competing Hellenistic mystery cults, the church survived because of the Spirit of loyalty and love that stood as the living trace of the risen Lord.

The primitive church, as shaped by the theology of Paul, developed three fundamental ideas that have frequently been distorted or misinterpreted by the subsequent tradition. The first idea is that the salvation of the individual comes only from membership in the right kind of community. Second, the individual is subject to an intrinsic moral burden that cannot be overcome without divine agency. According to the third idea, salvation is only through the Atonement. This Atonement is the inner meaning of Jesus' utterances about the Kingdom of Heaven. Royce takes pains to rethink these ideas in such a way as to free them from the sedimentation of tradition. The Pauline Epistles transform the hermeneutically opaque sayings of the founder to articulate these three insights in a binding and universalizable manner. A dialectical relation between Paul and his primitive churches provides the structural clearing within which these ideas unfold. Central to all three ideas is Royce's fundamental ethical and religious principle of loyalty.

Royce insists that his work in *The Problem of Christianity* is continuous with his earlier work, especially his ethics of loyalty as presented in 1908. In his 1913 formulation, loyalty receives a religious extension, and Royce defines Christianity as the religion of loyalty.

> But the depth and vitality of the ideal of loyalty have become better known to me as I have gone on with my work. Each of my efforts to express what I have found in the course of my study of what loyalty means has contained, as I believe, some new results. My efforts to grasp and to expound the "religion of loyalty" have at length led me, in this book, to views concerning the essence of Christianity such that, if they have any truth, they need to be carefully considered.[1]

The Spirit of loyalty, as exemplified above all in Paul, is central to an understanding of genuine community. For Royce, Christianity comes closer than any other major religion to expressing the Spirit of loyalty as it works itself out in the Beloved Community of the body of Christ. Loyalty is both an ethical and a religious notion and refers above all to the healthy functioning of the community as composed of loyal selves.

Royce extends his claims for the importance of loyalty by insisting that the community cannot survive without it. Loyalty is the practical element of love preserved in the community.

> If indeed I myself must cry "out of the depths" before the light can come to me, it must be my Community that, in the end, saves me. To assert this and to live this doctrine constitutes the very core of the Christian experience, and of the "Religion of Loyalty." . . . When I now say that by loyalty I mean the practically devoted love of an individual for a community, I shall

---

[1]Josiah Royce, *The Problem of Christianity*, ed. John E. Smith (Chicago: University of Chicago Press, 1968) 38. Subsequent citations are noted in the text and refer to this edition.

leave unenlightened those who stop short at the purely verbal fact that the
word *community* also ends in *ty*. (41)

Loyalty cements the communal bonds by keeping love alive. The loyal self
hopes to preserve and enlarge the role of the community in private experience. This is essential to the interpretive process and the quest to understand other selves both within the community and within alien
communities.

Yet it is not enough to discuss the essential traits of loyalty as if it were
an atemporal experience. Royce immediately raises the historical question regarding the earliest complete expression of loyalty. Throughout the
text, there exists a certain tension between the essential and the historical. No understanding of the essential traits of loyalty or community is
adequate if it is not accompanied by a historical analysis of the development of those traits in human history. For Royce, this analysis entails a
detailed study of early Christianity and the emergent doctrine of the
Christ.

Christianity is seen as the premier religion of loyalty. To fully grasp
this view, however, requires a study of the earliest stages of this religion,
which in turn entails a historical analysis of the founder and his teachings, as well as how these teachings were received by the primitive church.
Royce directs attention away from the biography of Jesus toward the
metaphysical presuppositions that guided the early church.

> Historically speaking, Christianity has never appeared simply as the reli-
> gion taught by the Master. It has always been an interpretation of the Mas-
> ter and of his religion in the light of some doctrine concerning his mission,
> and also concerning God, man, and man's salvation,—a doctrine which,
> even in its simplest expressions, has always gone beyond what the Master
> himself is traditionally reported to have taught while he lived. (66)

Royce refuses to identify Christianity with the simple pietism of Jesus and
his life. Rather, the hermeneutic problem appears at the start of his analysis when he insists that the Master is in some fundamental sense a product of the subsequent metaphysical interpretations of his life and work.
Thus Royce is concerned with the Jesus of the historical church rather than
the Jesus of history. The early church created the interpretation of Jesus
and his mission, and Paul partook in this creation and added his own genius to the interpretations then current.

Royce works through his hermeneutic problematic on several levels.
On one level he addresses the historical question concerning the specific
interpretations made by the Pauline community as it wrestled with the
meaning of the life of Jesus. This approach entails an analysis of the metaphysics animating the primitive church and of Paul's own addition to this
metaphysics. On another level, Royce raises anew the general hermeneutic problem of the nature of interpretation and its essential traits. On
yet another level, Royce tries to articulate the final horizon within which

hermeneutics moves. Here he broadens his metaphysics of community to articulate the workings of the community of interpretation. It is important to note that these three levels of analysis often interpenetrate and illuminate each other. Thus, for example, Paul's understanding of the Beloved Community as the body of Christ sheds light on the more general nature of the community of interpretation. Or, again, the Peircean understanding of the act of interpretation (in its ahistorical guise) illuminates how the primitive church used the doctrine of the Holy Spirit to understand mediation of viewpoints.

This codependence of analysis must be kept in view. Royce developed his hermeneutics from both the generic/essential and the particular/historical perspectives. The historical material—for example, his analysis of the doctrine of Atonement—is grasped with the aid of his general theory of interpretation. The essential material is understood from his analysis of the hermeneutic principles of the primitive church. Neither perspective should take absolute or systematic priority.

Royce is concerned with showing how the primitive church was faced with the problem of interpretation. Specifically, it asked, how are the sayings of Jesus to be understood and applied? The problem is compounded by the fact that Jesus did not provide hermeneutic guidelines for understanding his utterances. Hence the early church was forced to develop such guidelines on its own. Royce states the problem thus:

> Since these later interpretations have to do with matters that the original sayings and parables, so far as reported, leave more or less problematic, so as to challenge further inquiry; and since all these more problematic matters are indeed of central importance for the whole estimate of the Christian doctrine of life, we may indeed have to recognize that the primitive Christianity of the sayings of the Master was both enriched and deepened by the interpretation which the Christian community gave to his person, to his work, and to his whole religion. (69)

Jesus did not provide enough conceptual material for the proper understanding of his life and works. Royce rejects the view that we must return to the life of Jesus to understand the "true" meaning of Christianity. Rather, we must look to the early church and its process of elaborating the enigmatic and incomplete oral material. Of course, the texts themselves emerged out of the early church as it struggled to understand the oral tradition. Without the hermeneutic manipulations of the community, the tradition could not have survived in the long run. Hence Royce seats the locus of Christianity in the hermeneutic acts of the primitive church.

Royce goes further in his historical study by articulating the specific hermeneutic choices of the primitive church. He sees the central teaching of Jesus as the preaching of the Kingdom of Heaven. From this primitive core the early church developed its theological articulation. The church believed that the Spirit aided its hermeneutic manipulations and helped it to see the deeper meanings in the words of Jesus. According to Royce,

> They are all of them ideas that came to the mind of the Christian world in the course of later efforts to explain the true meaning of the original teaching regarding the Kingdom of Heaven. The Christian community regarded them as due to the guidance of the founder's spirit; but it was also aware that, when they first came to light, they involved new features, which the reported sayings and parables of the Master had not yet made so explicit as they afterwards became. (70)

These ideas about the meaning of the Kingdom of Heaven went beyond the utterances attributed to the historical founder. His Spirit became the self-understood guide of the community in its quest for fuller understanding. Outside his abiding Spirit, the teachings could not have become actual in the historical community.

Royce, as noted, singles out three of the ideas derived from the core teaching of the Kingdom of Heaven: the Beloved Community, the moral burden of the individual, and the Atonement. Together these ideas represent the framework for the early church.

Jesus, by dying on the cross and rising again through the Resurrection, atones for the sin of the first man (Adam) and makes it possible for the Beloved Community to follow. This Beloved Community forms the moral matrix within which the individual can find his or her way toward the loyalty that overcomes the weight and burden of sin. Outside the community, as the body of Christ, the individual is unable to overcome the moral burden of sin.

The Spirit, emergent from the life and death of Jesus, forms the foundation for those moral acts that realize community. The Beloved Community of the faithful is the grace-filled center of the Universal Community of all humankind. The Kingdom of Heaven resides not in the end of history but in the loyal members of the community. Royce thus insists that the Kingdom is alive among the members and is in search of greater historical and physical expression. While the actual churches might not manifest the Kingdom, the invisible church is its home.

Returning to his 1908 formulation of the philosophy of loyalty, Royce gives concrete expression to the individual's relation to both the visible and the invisible church. This loyalty, while seeking universal expression, must receive its initial articulation in the given local community. This particular community is seen to have many traits analogous to a person and to thereby become worthy of loyalty and love.

> One's family, one's circle of personal friends, one's home, one's village community, one's clan, or one's country may be the object of such an active disposition to love and serve the community as a unity, to treat the community as if it were a sort of super-personal being, and as if it could, in its turn, possess the value of a person on some higher level. . . . I know

of no better name for such a spirit of active devotion to the community to which the devoted individual belongs, than the excellent old word "Loyalty." (82-83)

These particular and local communities form the initial place in which loyalty, as essentially religious emotion or act, can function. Yet this loyalty is not confined to the given local community. Loyalty is a generic stance. It seeks the Universal Community as its final home.

There does remain, however, a tension between the need for a local setting and the drive for a universal one. In his 1908 article entitled "Provincialism," Royce stresses the necessity of local customs and mores. In giving his own definition of *province*, he intrudes honorific notions as to its value.

For me, then, a province shall mean any one part of a national domain, which is, geographically and socially, sufficiently unified to have a true consciousness of its own ideals and customs, and to possess a sense of its distinction from other parts of the country. And by the term "provincialism" I shall mean, first, the tendency of such a province to possess its own customs and ideals; secondly, the totality of these customs and ideals themselves; and thirdly, the love and pride which leads the inhabitants of a province to cherish as their own these traditions, beliefs, and aspirations.[2]

The province is thus the seat of all values and proper aspirations. Outside of such a province, we are led to conclude, only meaninglessness can occur. Within it our spiritual horizon is secure.

Royce goes even further by insisting that the province, and its attendant attitude of provincialism, is the basic political and social life. By reviving provincialism we can cure the ills of our time. In the same 1908 article he makes this striking claim: "My thesis is that, in the present state of the world's civilization, and of the life of our own country, the time has come to emphasize, with a new meaning and intensity, the positive value, the absolute necessity for our own welfare, of a wholesome provincialism, as a saving power to which the world in the near future will need more and more to appeal."[3] This "wholesome provincialism" is recommended for all persons, whatever their national affiliations. Furthermore, national life itself is derived from healthy provincial life. The province provides the individual with the initial object of loyalty. It provides the hermeneutic paradigm within which the loyal individual will understand reality. Thought and language are, or should be, bound to the province. Interpretive acts derive their initial validation from the province. Hermeneutics is thus guided, at least on this level of analysis, by the conceptual structures of the province.

---

[2]Josiah Royce, *Basic Writings*, ed. John J. McDermott, 2 vols. (Chicago: University of Chicago Press, 1969) 2:1069.

[3]Ibid.

As noted, Royce's universalism remains in tension with this provincialism. Loyalty needs a concrete basis in our hermeneutic acts. Yet this basis is not to be used dogmatically. Royce resolves the tension between the particular and the universal by showing the deeper meaning of both loyalty and interpretation. While we must first be loyal to a province, which entails following its interpretive guidelines, we must secondly realize that true loyalty seeks to protect and nurture the loyalty of other individuals and provinces.

Loyalty is thus both particular and universal. It is the quest for the Universal Community, even though it springs from the love of one's family or clan. The Universal Community is to be loyally realized in the ideal future. The inner logic of loyalty is to achieve wholeness of expression. "The logical development of the loyal spirit is therefore the rise of a consciousness of the ideal of an universal community of the loyal,—a community which, despite all warfare and jealousy, and despite all varieties of gods and laws, is supreme in its value, however remote from the present life of civilization" (84). Here Royce admits the presence of differing "gods and laws" yet insists that a loyal spirit produces a community that transcends these differences. This community, however, as the universal body of Christ, remains in the future. The Kingdom of Heaven is thus only partially attained. It is still a part of history, rather than its end, yet its full historical expression remains remote.

Loyalty, as envisioned by Royce, belongs with love. For Christianity the idea of a community of the loyal is derived from what both Jesus and Paul say about love. This love is not passive and weak but is heroic and strong. This love is directed to both God and one's neighbor. Jesus gave us a concrete understanding of the love of God for us in his own life and death. However, he failed to articulate a social framework in which the love for neighbors could function. For Royce, Paul helped us toward this social understanding of neighbor love by envisioning the Beloved Community as the body of Christ. This insight helped the church unite the love of God with the love of our neighbors and also concretized the preachings of Jesus. Royce states Paul's conception as follows: "This new being is a corporate entity,—the body of Christ, or the body of which the now divinely exalted Christ is the head. Of this body the exalted Christ is also, for Paul, the spirit and also, in some new sense, the lover. The corporate entity is the Christian community itself" (93). Paul was able to give some concrete direction to the general views on love as found in Jesus. Christ became the body of the living church, one guided by the Spirit of interpretation. However, without the central Pauline elaboration of the ethics of love, as found in the body of Christ, the message of Jesus would not have become historically effective.

Outside the Beloved Community one was condemned to live life under the power of the law. For Royce, the Pauline distinction between law and grace serves to illuminate the difference between life within the loyal community and life after the flesh in communities that are not touched by the interpretive Spirit or by the light of grace. Paul's "natural man" is the disloyal man and has not fully grasped the truth of self-consciousness, namely, that it emerges from the social contrasts that evidence a reality beyond the hubristic reach of the individual.

The hermeneutic choices of the primitive church address the specific problems that were left unanswered in the sayings of the founder. Jesus thus set the horizon for the problematic and even gave some indication regarding the proper direction for query. Yet it was the Pauline community that formed the historically effective framework for Christian ethics and theology. Again, Royce insists that we cannot fall back on a naive belief in the biographical and historical Jesus. Such a Jesus cannot provide sufficient grounding for dogmatics or ethics. Rather, we must find the Jesus who is largely the product of the early church in its struggles to provide the proper interpretation of the sayings.

Community is to be understood as being more concrete than the detached individual. It is a living and whole body, of which the individual is a mere part. The relation between the individual and the community is one of love. As Royce reads Paul, love is the most fully realized form of loyalty. Royce refers repeatedly to Paul's First Letter to the Corinthians, where this love is forcefully stated.

> If I speak in the tongues of men and of angels, but have not love, I am a noisy gong or a clanging cymbal. And if I have prophetic powers, and understand all mysteries and all knowledge, and if I have all faith, so as to remove mountains, but have not love, I am nothing. If I give away all I have, and if I deliver my body to be burned, but have not love, I gain nothing. (1 Cor. 13:1-3)

Royce interprets Paul's criticisms of prophecy as a critique of unbridled individualism and egoism. The Corinthians suffer from the Hellenistic bias toward special personal manifestations of the powers, and it is the role of the Beloved Community to redirect these false manifestations toward loyalty and love.

The community functions in a variety of ways to ensure that loyalty emerges in individuals. Individualism is tempered by the social conflict that produces moral awareness. This social control provides interpretive guidelines for our conscience. Hence the community, as the scene of intense conflict, gives us our moral self-appraisal. This is a hermeneutic task in that it gives us the parameters within which we are to interpret behavior as either good or bad. Such an awareness cannot come from introspection or private reflection. This view harks back to Peirce's criticisms of intuition and introspection as sources of knowledge. Royce's Paul reinforces these Peircean insights by showing just how the community functions in self-awareness.

Royce takes pains to show the concrete links between personal and social evaluation. We cannot hope to understand the meaning of our moral acts until we place them before the bar of the community. The interpretations thus derived will govern our future conduct. In Royce's view,

> The social environment that most awakens our self-consciousness about our conduct does so by opposing us, by criticising us, or by otherwise standing in contrast to us. Our knowledge of ourselves as the authors or as the guides of our conduct, our knowledge of how and why we do what we do,—all such more elaborate self-knowledge is, directly or indirectly, a social product, and a product of social contrasts and oppositions of one sort or another. Our fellows train us to all our higher grades of practical self-knowledge, and they do so by giving us certain sorts of social trouble. (107)

A social psychology underlies the moral theory in that our own conscience is a by-product of social interaction. The community functions to undermine the more extreme forms of individualism. It also gives us a growing sense of our moral burden insofar as we are guilty of a moral position that we ourselves cannot overcome. The community thus gives us our sense of sin and guilt.

Our sense of sin, and the concomitant need for atonement, is fostered by the outer law of the community. This law functions to sharpen our individuality by forcing us into the mode of rebellion. This tension produces our moral guilt. Royce asserts, "The more outer law is in our cultivation, the more inner rebellion there is in the very individuals whom our cultivation creates. And this moral burden of the individual is also the burden of the race, precisely in so far as it is a race that is social in a human sense" (116). Royce is not naive about the problems that can emerge from the relationships between the individual and the community. The very forces that produce the individual ego and its moral awareness are the forces that threaten it from without. The two extreme possibilities are excessive individualism and the act of true loyalty to the community. Our sense of sin comes from the possibility of betrayal of the community that brought our ego and individuality into being in the first place. The solution to this tension lies in the doctrine of loyalty, which serves to unite the individual to the community. The doctrine of the Atonement functions, as we shall see, in the postloyal phase in which an act of treason breaks the bonds of the Beloved Community.

Loyalty brings us to a new knowledge of the self and its community. We no longer know the world "after the flesh" but "after the Spirit." This new knowledge brings us beyond the moral burden that held us in its grip.

> Such human love knows its objects precisely as Paul declared that, henceforth, he would no longer know Christ,—namely, "after the flesh." Loyalty knows its object (if I may again adapt Paul's word) "after the Spirit." For Paul's expression here refers, in so far as he speaks of human objects at all, to the unity of the spirit which he conceived to be characteristic of the Christian community, whereof Christ was, to the Apostle's mind, both the head and the divine life. (126)

Loyalty carries with it a new type of knowledge with its own hermeneutic foundation in the Spirit. Yet the Spirit itself is a gift of grace that lies behind the new knowledge. Royce's doctrine of grace is central to his hermeneutics in that it enables the individual to go beyond the old knowledge after the flesh. Further, grace brings us more fully into the membership of the Beloved Community.

The Beloved Community is thus the place where the individual is purified of subjective hermeneutic distortions. The community comes to provide the proper mediating thirds for our specific interpretations. This Beloved Community is not a natural community of merely random individuals. It is intrinsically lovable and worthy of loyalty. As Royce comments,

> In order to be thus lovable to the critical and naturally rebellious soul, the Beloved Community must be, quite unlike a natural social group, whose life consists of laws and quarrels, of a collective will, and of individual rebellion. This community must be an union of members who first love it. This unity of love must pervade it, before the individual member can find it lovable. (129)

Without love and loyalty we cannot talk of genuine community. A merely natural community consists of the numerical sum of discrete selves. Love functions to solidify that random mass into one living body. Loyalty keeps these natural individuals from acting against the resultant community.

Royce contrasts Christianity with Buddhism and finds the latter wanting. Buddhism functions only to deny the blind strivings of the will. It cannot move beyond this negative stance to provide a justification for our ethical deeds. Christianity, by contrast, shows us the true loyalty that gives our finite deeds meaning in the flow of time and in the community. Royce sees Christianity as being more insightful into the nature of community and its needs than other religions. Chief among the achievements of Christianity is the discovery of the Spirit as the inner guide of the community's hermeneutic acts. The Spirit inspired and directed the primitive church in its quest for the meaning of God and the founder.

> But, historically speaking, Christianity has been distinguished by the concreteness and intensity with which, in the early stages of its growth, it grasped, loved, and served its own ideal of the visible community, supposed to be universal, which it called its Church. It has further been contrasted with other religions by the skill with which it gradually revised its views of the divine nature, in order to be able to identify the spirit that, as it believed, guided, inspired, and ruled this Church, with the spirit of the one whom it had come to worship as its risen Lord. (134-35)

The early Christian church (read as Pauline community) developed a metaphysically astute view of community and the role of the Spirit in its life. Royce makes the strong claim that Christianity has done so in an exemplary fashion. Buddhism, even with its great psychological insight, simply failed to find the proper view of the Universal Community. Furthermore, it had no conception of the loyalty that unites or of the Atonement that overcomes even treason. This raises an important problem for Royce's implied philosophy of religion. If the Christian church, especially in its early form, is a paradigm of all true religion, then Royce's quest for a universal community of the Beloved is weakened. This conclusion exhibits a tension in Royce that is not easily resolved. On the one hand he does not appear to be calling for a worldwide Christian confessional community, while on the other, he does seem to judge all other religions as incomplete or weak by his more robust Christian standards. Royce is not easily labeled a Christian chauvinist, even though his metaphysics remains tied to what could be loosely called a Christian framework. We will keep this tension in sight in what follows.

The Spirit was seen as the concrete guide for the rule of the church. The Spirit was also seen as being connected with the risen Lord. Without the constant presence of the Spirit, understood here as the Spirit of interpretation, the community could not have emerged from the simple story of the life and death of Jesus. The Spirit functions as the ultimate guide for all communal interpretations and conceptual elaborations of the meaning of the life and work of Jesus. For the mature Royce (after 1912), the community could not be fully understood without the doctrine of the Spirit as the moving presence of the risen Lord.

Royce's historical analysis thus makes two general statements about hermeneutics. First, the early church made a number of hermeneutic manipulations of the oral tradition to generate a rich view of the nature of community, God, and the meaning of the life and work of the founder. This claim accords with recent analyses of the role of the primitive church. Royce's denial of the importance of the biographical Jesus is also in line with most recent biblical scholarship. Second, the Spirit guided the early community in its hermeneutic manipulations. Without this Spirit the true meaning of Jesus' work would not have emerged. Together these two claims show the central role of interpretation in the genesis of Christianity.

Returning to the problem of loyalty, we see Royce affirming that the individual is often bereft of grace and the presence of Spirit. He deepens his grasp of the nature of sin qua disloyalty before introducing formally the doctrine of Atonement. For the Atonement can have no meaning outside of the deeds that require reconciliation with the loyal Spirit of the community.

The reality of the Atonement is not fully grasped in the traditional "penal satisfaction" view, which sees the Christ as having once and for all made the sacrifice that cancels sin and guilt. Royce argues that such a view would seem alien to the guilty person in search of personal reconciliation. The penal view reduces the Atonement to a tale of an angry God in search of personal satisfaction, willing thereby to sacrifice his own Son on the altar of history in order to rectify the divine/human transaction.

Contrasted to the penal view is what Royce calls the moral theory, which stresses our sympathetic and loving response to the life and work of Christ. Unlike the penal view, the moral view does not reduce to a form of business transaction in which an angry God receives payment for specific misdeeds. The moral view argues that sinful persons become reconciled to God when they learn to open their hearts to the loving death of the Christ. This conception of the Atonement extracts no payment and demands no satisfaction. Rather, it involves a warming of the heart through an emotional imitation of Jesus' love for us. This warming is not a metaphysical reconstitution of the human and divine worlds but a psychological transformation of present attitudes.

The parables of the New Testament, as read by Royce, do not give us any clues regarding which view of the Atonement is correct. However, the Pauline Epistles show us the inadequacies of the penal and moral views and present a third alternative that reaches to the heart of the life of sin and guilt. This third view, which we can call the Pauline view of the Atonement, is most clearly evident in the life of one particular, if untypical, member of the community.

Royce chooses an extreme example of disloyalty to pave the way for his understanding of atonement. His example is that of a traitor who does a deed so damaging to the community that it looks as if the community will not recover its former strength or power. This deed stands across time as something that cannot be erased. The traitor would give anything to blot this deed out of existence and out of communal memory. Whatever his efforts, however, this deed remains a scar on the body of the community. The deed cannot be revoked. The traitor consigns himself to this "hell of the irrevocable" in realizing that the deed stands forever (162).

This sharpening of the sense of the irrevocable prepares the way for the doctrine of the Atonement. The deed cannot be removed by the traitor, but a loyal servant of the community can appear who will produce a counterdeed that will overcome the damage of the first deed. This new loyal deed will actually enhance the community in such a way as to redeem both the evil deed and the traitor. Royce goes as far as to say that the community will be better off than if the evil deed had not occurred. In this sense the traitor will be atoned.

> And hereupon the new deed, as I suppose, is so ingeniously devised, so concretely practical in the good which it accomplishes, that, when you look down upon the human world after the new creative deed has been done in it, you say, first, "This deed was made possible by that treason; and secondly, the world, as transformed by this creative deed, is better than it would have been had all else remained the same, but had not the deed of treason been done at all." That is, the new creative deed has made the new world better than it was before the blow of treason fell. (180)

Put in more traditional language, we see here the notion that Christ atones for the sin of Adam and thus remakes and renews the world and all that is in it. The world is thus better off because the original sin or original state occurred. The disloyal traitor is brought back into the community of the loyal by the saving deed of the loyal servant. Of course, the primary loyal servant is Jesus, who atoned for our disloyalty in a metaphysically fundamental way. On the hermeneutic level we can say that the traitor is the one who has a totally misguided practical interpretation of reality. The traitor stands outside of the Spirit of interpretation that guides both the ethical and conceptual acts of the community. Hence, both our moral and intellectual isolation can be atoned for by the loyal community, which acts to bring us back to the body of Christ.

For Royce, God is directly interested in bringing us back into the community as expressed in the premier symbol of the kingdom of Heaven.

> For God's love towards the individual is, from the Christian point of view, a love for one whose destiny it is to be a member of the Kingdom of Heaven. The Kingdom of Heaven is essentially a community. And the idea of this community, as the founder in parables prophetically taught that idea, developed into the conception which the Christian Church formed of its own mission; and through all changes, and despite all human failures, this conception remains a sovereign treasure of the Christian world. (193)

Our sins, both moral and intellectual, are atoned for in the love of God, which brings us back to the loyal community. God's love functions to guide us back to the interpretations of the world that have the greatest approximation to the truth. The doctrine of the Atonement shows just how God's love functions for us. By participating in the unearned atonement, the traitor is (and, by implication, we are) brought back to the proper practical interpretation of the problematic situation. Hence the Atonement serves a pragmatic hermeneutics of the moral self.

As always in Royce, the Atonement functions to bring the individual back into the reality of the community. The hermeneutic import is obvious in that the individual is now in a position to move beyond private categorical and practical projections and enter into the more "truthful" communal reality. An interesting recent use of the notion of the saving power of the community can be seen in H. Richard Niebuhr's *Christ and Culture*, where specific references to Royce and his conception of loyalty can be found. According to Niebuhr,

> Faith is a dual bond of loyalty and trust that is woven around the members of such a community. It does not issue from a subject simply; it is called forth as trust by acts of loyalty on the part of others; it is infused as loyalty to a cause by others who are loyal to that cause and to me. Faith exists only in a community of selves in the presence of a transcendent cause.[4]

---

[4]H. Richard Niebuhr, *Christ and Culture* (New York: Harper & Row, 1951) 253.

Niebuhr uses Royce's view in order to conclude his own account of culture and Christianity. Niebuhr relies on the Roycean analysis of the Christian community to attack the existentialist overemphasis on the individual in isolation. Outside the loyal community it is impossible for the individual to find the atonement that will enable him or her to overcome the specific moral burden of being human.

Royce foreshadows Niebuhr with his insistence that private piety and mysticism are alone insufficient to encompass the religious life. His general admiration for Meister Eckhart is modified so as to allow for the social dimension of Christianity. "Of this I am sure: Mystical piety can never either exhaust or express the whole Christian doctrine of life. For the Christian doctrine of life, in its manifoldness, in the intensity and variety of human interests to which it appeals, is an essentially social doctrine. Private individual devotion can never justly interpret it" (216). Hence so-called private party religion is rejected in favor of the public and communal expression of the realized life in the body of Christ. The communal and ethical doctrines serve to provide a foundation for the hermeneutic doctrines in both their historical and essential forms.

This religious community, the Beloved Community, is somewhat akin to the Absolute of the pre-1912 writings. In fact, Royce even hints that the community is itself divine. "Man the community may prove to be God, as the traditional doctrine of Christ, of the Spirit, and of the Church seem to imply. But all such possible outcomes and interpretations, to which the Christian doctrine of life may lead, must be discovered for themselves" (220). The ontological conclusion of the extended analysis of the nature of Christianity is that persons are fully defined only in communal terms and that the community, especially when seen as the body of Christ, may be divine. This position seems to imply a divination of persons not unlike that found in post-Kantian idealism. God becomes embedded in and manifest through the communal structures that govern personal life. For Royce, this is the true meaning of the incarnation.

The divinity of the community, whether that of the community of interpretation or that of the Beloved Community, provides the meaning horizon within which human life prevails. In chapter 3, we considered the differences between communal orders and the other orders of nature. We found that human communities, unlike prehuman aggregates, are constituted by the traits of temporality, self-reflection, and intersubjectivity. The development of self-consciousness requires that these three dimensions of communal transaction become manifest in the life of the individual. Whenever a community allows for the presence of the Spirit-Interpreter, it becomes a locus for the incarnation. The problem of the divinity of communal orders must now be extended to the larger problem of all of the orders of nature. In what sense can we extend the notion of

the incarnation beyond human interpretive communities? More point-
edly, where is the incarnation, and what are its limits, if any? The answer
to these questions can come only from a more careful analysis of the prehuman orders and their bearing on the human.

To make progress in this area we must return to another American
tradition that has shed a great deal of light on the problem of the divini-
zation of nature. In particular, we must examine the thought of Emerson,
who inverted the usual understanding of the correlation between text and
nature in such a way as to make nature itself the primary text of human
life. Emerson's decentralizing of the Judeo-Christian Bible and his con-
sequent elevation of the spiritual presence of the orders of extrahuman
nature represent one of the most fundamental realignments in human
thought. In chapter 5, we will see how this shift gives us a more encompassing perspective within which to locate both Royce's hermeneutic
project and the more generic project of horizonal hermeneutics. Animating and governing the community of interpretation is the sheer Providingness of nature itself, which is the ultimate enabling condition for our
interpretive lives.

Royce, as we saw in chapter 1, argued that nature itself was an interpretive process and that some rudimentary sense of sign function must
prevail in the innumerable orders of the world. These precommunal orders stand as the enabling condition for all hermeneutic transactions. This
is not to argue, of course, that nature is fundamentally mental but that
some kind of interpretive process must operate between complexes that
are preconscious. While nature cannot exemplify the traits of temporality, self-reflection, and intersubjectivity, it must have some traits that facilitate the interpretive process on both the prehuman and human levels.
Only a hermeneutics artificially limited to the paradigm of human written texts will ignore the impulses that come from a nature with its own
valid meaning structures. Do we thus argue that nature is a sign process
and that causal and other transactions are semiotic through and through?
As we noted in chapter 1, some interpretations of Peirce move in this direction and see nature as being the sum of all actual and possible signs.
This conceptual move is invariably facilitated by an implied or stated
panpsychism that sees matter as merely one type of mind. Thinkers as
diverse as Leibniz, Whitehead, and Hartshorne have been sympathetic
to this extension of the notion of mentality to prehuman complexes. Perhaps there is another way to come to grips with the interpretive dimension of nature without extending such metaphysical license to the traits
of mentality.

I devote part of chapter 5 to showing the status of the incarnation and
the Spirit in those orders of the world that support human community.
Emerson's discovery of the inner logic of natural processes represents a

turning that determines the deeper trajectory of the history of hermeneutics. The measure for our Bible comes not only from the primitive church and its articulation in the writings of Paul but in the indefinitely ramified orders of Spirit-filled nature. The living human community and the communal orders of nature together determine the shape of all our interpretive transactions. But the true depth dimension of these transactions can be found only in nature, which gives meaning to all life.

FROM THE NATURE
OF COMMUNITY TO THE
COMMUNITY OF NATURE

Human interpretive communities are not discontinuous with nature, any more than any complex can become detached from its ordinal placement. The inner power of the hermeneutic community is the agency of the Spirit, which quickens each interpretation and makes it transparent to other interpreters and to the world from which it has come and toward which it points. No sign relation can be detached from its natural locations and its specific history within given communities. The content of the community (its innumerable signs and sign systems) and the form of the community (its interpretive matrix) both receive their possibility and meaning from the vast domain of a nature that was neither made nor formed by the community. The contemporary emphasis on the manipulative dimension of human interpretation ignores the more fundamental dimension of assimilation, in which nature is endured and encountered without benefit of prior human definition or analysis. The shocks of rudimentary experience testify to the sheer prevalence of a nature that is forever just beyond the reach of our hermeneutic acts.

The community of interpretation can be understood to be a categorical and semiotic clearing that represents the opening power of the human over the orders of nature. Nature becomes unhidden within the hermeneutic community that gives it a "place" within which to become articulate and, if we may stretch the analogy, self-conscious. Outside of human communities, nature would be only dimly illuminated through fitful and nonreflexive animal consciousness. Of course, the teeming realms of animal consciousness function as rudimentary clearings onto nature and world, even if the clearings themselves lack generic spread and interpretive complexity. We must avoid anthropocentric bias when moving toward a just account of the nature of the hermeneutic power of prehuman complexes. In moving from an account of community to an account of nature, the priority of the human must be balanced by a sensitivity to the more general traits of a nature that manifests a striking drive toward both self-overcoming and self-transparency.

In our analysis of Royce and the community of interpretation, we concluded with the insight that the incarnation can be found to be active in the Spirit of the hermeneutic community. In what follows I wish to show how the incarnation functions within the prehuman orders of nature. A few more general notions will be introduced by way of making this transition possible. Within the American tradition, the writings of Ralph Waldo Emerson hold a special priority. His decentralizing of the Bible and of textuality enabled him to show in an epoch-making manner how the Spirit works within nature and human genius to stabilize and enrich the human process. We will examine his 1836 work *Nature* in order to exhibit more clearly this transition from sacred text to the divinity of nature as the ultimate text. This conceptual and experiential realignment will in turn provide the historical justification for our concluding remarks about the status of the interpretive community within the orders of a Spirit-filled nature.

A certain tension exists between the notion of a unified Spirit and the notion of innumerable spirits, each representing something fundamental about the order in which it prevails. Theologically, no monotheism remains free from the temptation of a robust polytheism. Is this temptation always to be resisted, or can it be understood in a different way? Can the Spirit, as the agency and power of the incarnation through time and space, allow for a self-splintering so that its efficacy is enhanced rather than diminished? Or is this self-diremption merely on the level of appearance and not on that of reality? Put in another way, where is the incarnation and what is its inner principle of unity?

We begin to answer these questions when we recognize that the principle of unity does not entail singleness of expression, even if it does entail singleness of goal. The Spirit prevails in many discontinuous orders and can express itself in an ofttimes blinding array. These expressions serve to enhance and enrich the orders within which they occur. At the same time, they serve the larger ideal of unity insofar as they point toward a convergence that speaks from the fragmented orders themselves. This unity is not that of an atemporal perfection but that of a harmony within difference in which each natural order expresses the presence of the incarnation. The goal of the Spirit is toward the unity in which all of the finite expressions of Spirit receive their deeper measure in the incarnation. The interpretive community serves this Spirit when it recognizes that all finite spirits are moments of difference within the evolving and agapistic life of the true Spirit.

If, following Heidegger, we speak of an identity within difference, then we must allow that the realms of finite spirit serve to broaden the scope of the Spirit, without falling prey to a static principle of mere trait continuity.

Each spirit must be granted autonomy insofar as such autonomy is deepened by an eventual theonomy. An autonomous spirit becomes theonomous when it "recognizes" that its measure or law comes from a dimension outside itself and that this higher measure does not cancel but radicalizes autonomy. In the theonomous moment the spirit learns of its inner continuity with the Spirit that lies within all of the complexes of nature.

The connection between finite spirits is best characterized as a feeling of feeling in which one spirit feels the presence and power of another. Whitehead coined the technical term *prehension* to represent this feeling or state of attunement that reaches across the spirits to sustain unity. For human interpretive communities, prehension operates on the conscious level in sign series. A given sign or series prehends another insofar as it lets it become relevant to it either weakly or strongly. This process is conscious and deliberate whenever finite interpreters seek to expand the scope of their hermeneutic acts. On the precommunal and prehuman levels, prehension is rarely, if ever, conscious. It is indeed, as Whitehead argues, a feeling for another feeling. Throughout nature, prehensive attunement functions as the unifying power between complexes. Of course, discontinuity and nonrelevance are as much a part of nature as are continuity and connection. Whitehead erred in insisting that each complex (his "actual occasion") prehends every other. While prehension links any complex to some others, it does not link all complexes into one atemporal unit.

Finite spirits, as ultimately rooted in the Spirit itself, prehend each other insofar as they become theonomous. Of course, we are using anthropomorphic language where it is often inappropriate. All discourse about spirits must be metaphorical. Emerson, more than a decade before he wrote his first book, *Nature*, gives voice to the correlation between the gods (finite spirits) and human imagination.

> He who wanders in the woods perceives how natural it was to pagan imagination to find gods in every grove & by each fountain head. Nature seems to him not to be silent but to be eager and striving to break out into music. Each tree, flower, and stone, he invests with life & character; and it is impossible that the wind which breathes so expressive a sound amid the leaves—should mean nothing.[1]

Nature drives toward expression and meaning. Human imagination enhances this process by clothing each complex with a god or spirit that seems to embody the essential traits of that complex. Is this process arbitrary and hopelessly anthropocentric? Emerson would argue that the investment made by the imagination uses human characteristics to articulate traits in nature

---

[1]Ralph Waldo Emerson, *Emerson in His Journals*, ed. Joel Porte (Cambridge: Harvard University Press, 1982) 15.

that mirror the human. These traits are prehended by the poet in such a way as to show their continuity with the symbolic realm of the human process. The evocation of the spirits is anthropomorphic only insofar as it takes forms that prefigure human reality and gives them a human contour. In a very real sense, this process is not arbitrary. In fact, it reverses the anthropocentric dilemma by showing how human traits are slumbering in a nature rife with meaning and expression.

Turning to Emerson's *Nature,* we can trace in some detail his decentralizing of sacred texts in order to give priority to a nature that embodies all of the fundamental truths of those texts without their attendant provincial distortions. The status of his anthropomorphism can be best illuminated through an understanding of the role of Spirit in linking nature and humanity.

Emerson firmly rejects the traditional Augustinian notion of original sin, even though he retains some muted understanding of the Fall. This Fall is not from a state of obedience or from a divinely ordered covenant but from an original relation to the universe that contained its own self-validating revelation. This original relation allowed the power of the Spirit to permeate and govern the human process. Jesus, for Emerson little more than a representative man, served to express this relation in his life and teaching. Emerson ignores the Crucifixion in favor of a romantic evocation of the creative and poetic powers of the founder of Christianity. Insofar as we can imitate the spiritual power of the founder, we can become divinized ourselves.

The traits of the Fall are manifest whenever individuals allow the power of the horizon to recede from view so that finite and particular vistas prevail. The concept of horizon is, of course, both literal and metaphorical. Emerson has both dimensions in mind. "Miller owns this field, Locke that, and Manning the woodland beyond. But none of them owns the landscape. There is a property in the horizon which no man has but he whose eye can integrate all the parts, that is, the poet. This is the best part of these men's farms, yet to this their warranty-deeds give no title."[2] We have fallen from the liberating power of the horizon that enables us to integrate and order the realms of nature at our disposal. It is important to note that the horizon is not merely the static limit of our eye but it exerts a lure over our finite perspectives so that they may overcome their self-encapsulation. Emerson hints that economic interests blunt the drive of the human spirit toward the encompassing perspective that will locate and measure all subaltern perspectives. These interests can be transcended only when we are transformed by a spiritual presence that comes from a source outside human history and creativity.

---

[2]Ralph Waldo Emerson, *Nature, Addresses, and Lectures* (Boston: Houghton, Mifflin, 1883) 14. Subsequent citations are noted in the text and refer to this edition.

The imagery of circles and the human eye recur in a variety of contexts. The shape of the eye is a microcosmic analogue to the encompassing sweep of the horizon. The recurrence of fundamental moral patterns, in a cycle of action and reaction, gives the circular motif another dimension. In an oft-celebrated passage, Emerson uses this imagery to express a mystical experience.

> There I feel that nothing can befall me in life,—no disgrace, no calamity (leaving me my eyes), which nature cannot repair. Standing on the bare ground,—my head bathed by the blithe air, and uplifted into infinite space,—all mean egotism vanishes. I become a transparent eye-ball; I am nothing; I see all; the currents of the Universal Being circulate through me; I am part or parcel of God. (15-16)

The ego can be likened to a small circle that attempts to be its own horizon and that encloses the self upon itself in defiance of the spiritual energies that govern the universe. The power of the ego, as the topologist of an ever-shrinking empire, is broken only by the "currents" that animate the moral universe. Emerson argued throughout that the laws of physics were simply a material expression of the laws of moral compensation, laws that themselves obey the principle of action and reaction. The last clause in the quotation shows the utter radicalness of Emerson's perspective. Going beyond his fellow Unitarians, he affirms an identity between the poet, who now eclipses the priest in cultural and moral importance, and the God who sustains the poet in his or her creative enterprise. The genius/poet is the only true analogue to God the creator. Nature is incomplete until the poet finishes God's creation through spiritual works that house the Spirit in language.

Given the identity between the poet and God, it is easy to see why Emerson inverts the Christian understanding of the correlation between sacred text and nature. Nature, as the outer form of Spirit, contains all moral and religious truths and presents them in a form that is universal and free from the cultic and tribal limitations of the biblical writers. The very power of the biblical witness is a function of its ability to imitate through metaphor the spiritual truths of nature. The sacred texts of other traditions, many of which were carefully studied by Emerson in translation, stand in the same relation to a nature that gives birth to all religions and all moral perspectives. Indeed, the Judeo-Christian Bible is but a pale reflection of the truths found throughout the orders of nature.

Nature is the ultimate text and as such needs an interpreter who will be worthy of the complexities hidden within it. Religions, whether natural or positive, derive their power and value from the Spirit that is the animating core of an ever-fluid nature. According to Emerson, "Therefore is Nature ever the ally of Religion: lends all her pomp and riches to the religious sentiment. Prophet and priest, David, Isaiah, Jesus, have drawn deeply from this source. This ethical character so penetrates the bone and marrow of nature, as to seem the end for which it was made"(46).

The prophets locate the power of the Spirit in a moral nature that transcends the kingships that seem to usurp the power of God. Their protests against the broken covenant stem from strong moral intuitions that receive their outward expression through metaphors and similes drawn from nature. One has only to recall the words of Amos or Hosea to see the correctness of Emerson's observation.

> *But let justice roll down like waters,*
>   *and righteousness like an everflowing stream.* (Amos 5:24).
>
> *Therefore they shall be like the morning mist*
>   *or like the dew that goes early away,*
> *like the chaff that swirls from the threshing floor*
>   *or like smoke from a window.* (Hosea 13:3)

The unrighteous are in violation not only of the original covenant but of the very laws of nature that form the foundation for God's specific relationship with Israel and her kings. The inner logic of Judaism and of Christianity is found in the natural imagery that forms the moral and religious core of the Bible.

The relocating of sacred Scripture as merely one of innumerable expressions of the Spirit within nature entails a shift to aesthetic categories. The Beautiful is the ground for the Good and can be best rendered through works of art that support moral and religious truths through integral formal expression. The form of a work of art is analogous to the forms within nature that serve to order and govern local scenes. Emerson states,

> The ancient Greeks called the world *cosmos,* beauty. Such is the constitution of all things, or such the plastic power of the human eye, that the primary forms, as the sky, the mountain, the tree, the animal, give us a delight in and for themselves, a pleasure arising from outline, color, motion, and grouping. This seems partly owing to the eye itself. The eye is the best of artists. By the mutual action of its structures and of the laws of light, perspective is produced, which integrates every mass of objects, of what character soever, into a well colored and shaded globe, so that where the particular objects are mean and unaffecting, the landscape which they compose is round and symmetrical. (21)

Form, which is both imposed by the eye as the primary artist and discovered within nature, is an end in itself and not reducible to a mere means. In itself it grants repose to the soul in search of spiritual harmony and peace. Emerson deepens and radicalizes the traditional argument from design by insisting that natural and human products form symmetrical and rounded structures that attest to the presence of the Spirit both within the ramified orders of mute nature and within human contrivance. Spiritual peace comes from acts that locate the objects of vision within rounded horizons that grant and secure the repose of the Beautiful. No object is intrinsically devoid of beauty, even if it seems to contain local and regional traits of limited import and integrity. The nonbeautiful becomes transformed and transfixed whenever it is brought into harmony with a light-filled horizon. Implied in this argument is the claim that proper horizonal placement, what Emerson calls "a well colored and shaded globe," redeems finite particulars and shows their tendency toward radiance and transcendence. Redemption is no longer a religious category but belongs to the aesthetic realm.

The principle of unity joins with the principle of human creativity to show that nature itself is in need of the unifying acts of the artist if its richness and full contour are to become actualized. To be isolated from the seedbed of nature is to be bereft of the redemptive power that comes from the Spirit that achieves its fulfillment only in human spiritual acts. Emerson brings these themes together in this striking passage:

> Nothing is quite beautiful alone; nothing but is beautiful in the whole. A single object is only so far beautiful as it suggests this universal grace. The poet, the painter, the sculptor, the musician, the architect, seek each to concentrate this radiance of the world on one point, and each in his several work to satisfy the love of beauty which stimulates him to produce. Thus is Art a nature passed through the alembic of man. Thus in art does Nature work through the will of a man filled with the beauty of her first works. (29)

The radiance of the world is brought into its proper moment of abiding through the spiritual energies of the artist who serves to concentrate and unify the spiritual energies that animate the prehuman orders of nature. That nature is incomplete and in need of a second creation is a fundamental tenet of the transcendentalist creed. Of all the artists, the poet assumes preeminence in that the power of language encompasses the power of all other media of aesthetic transformation. Spirit is best housed in the poetic judgments that make communication possible. We need not return to the writings of the ancients, whether Greek or Hebrew, in order to find the power of Spirit within our own speech. Revelation and redemption are not confined to any given body of Scripture nor limited to one historical period. All of the power of the prophets and the wisdom of the Gospels can be encompassed in one intimate encounter with nature. For Emerson, bibliocentrism is a form of idolatry in which the Spirit is compressed into one body of expression. To so limit the efficacy and presence of the Spirit is to deaden the aesthetic impulses that ground and enliven religion.

Emerson's crisis of vocation over the Unitarian ministry was not simply a product of theological shifts. Of course, the rise of higher criticism in Germany, as conveyed to him by his brother, served to undermine the Unitarian belief in miracles that functioned to sustain the historical claims of his tradition. But more important than theological and historical-critical revolutions was the growing power of nature and its metaphorical enhancement through poetry. Emerson in effect rewrote the biblical witness so as to enhance its poetic evocation of natural and spiritual energies. His demythologization was motivated not so much by historiography as by the drive to return to a revelation that was not muted or blunted by myths or narratives of limited scope and sensitivity.

This shift from a Christian bibliocentric position to a truly universalist and aesthetic stance did not, however, induce Emerson simply to abandon the revelatory power of the Bible. It would be more accurate to say that the transcendentalist revolt struggled to liberate the biblical witness from an inadequate and provincial understanding of its message and fundamental direction. Emerson continued to affirm that the Judeo-Christian texts served to illuminate the human process and its inevitable and compulsive relation to the Divine. But it did not follow from this position that other texts and other human aesthetic products could not be equally effective in housing the Spirit in language or other media of incarnation. We can best understand Emerson's project if we see it as attempting to relocate and redefine human texts, whether inspired or not, within the infinite realm of nature toward which all texts point. Bibliocentrism masks a deeper poverty of Spirit that legislates in advance when and where the Spirit may become efficacious and present. Nature, as the ultimate text by which all others are judged and found wanting, has no boundary or regional limitations. Only nature, in its indefinite scope and complexity, can be a worthy home for the ever-elusive and protean Spirit.

If nature is the text of texts, then it becomes crucial to determine how we can have access to it in a way that best serves its own intrinsic meanings. How can human language picture or imitate the hidden language of nature? Can human utterance evoke and house the Spirit within nature, or must it forever remain but a pale imitation of that which transcends its reach? Emerson insists that language is not merely part of the realm of human convention and manipulation but that it has emerged from our encounters with a nature that has its own intrinsic meanings and expressions. Language rides on the back of nature and gives it utterance.

In the fourth chapter of *Nature* Emerson develops his view of language and its relation to nature. His analysis echoes the medieval belief in *analogia entis* and attempts to show that spiritual truths are part of the internal web of natural orders. He argues as follows:

> 1. Words are signs of natural facts. 2. Particular natural facts are symbols of particular spiritual facts. 3. Nature is the symbol of spirit. (31)

Emerson's semiotic drives directly toward the orders of nature and locates all signs within a nature/language transaction that is both transparent and open-ended. In our everyday use of language we often forget that moral and spiritual language derived its original meaning from its direct

reference to natural states of affairs. Emerson gives the following exam-
ples. The word *spirit* derives from our experience with the wind. The word
right derives from any movement across a terrain that is straight and does
not involve deviation. And the word *transgression* derives from our experience of crossing a line, whether natural or artifactual. All moral and
religious terminology can be traced back to fairly straightforward encounters with the proximate environment.

Of deeper import is his second claim that natural facts are symbols of
spiritual facts. In the contemporary preoccupation with written texts, little attention has been paid to the more traditional notion that nature itself
may embody meanings that are fairly precise and communicable. Perhaps
the fundamental spiritual truth that Emerson saw embodied in nature is
that of compensation, referred to above. Every action, in addition to its
obvious causal efficacy, evokes an equal and opposite reaction that serves
to measure and order its impact on the larger environment. On the physical level, this law has become a cornerstone of physical descriptions of
interaction. Yet Emerson saw this principle as the superficial analogue to
the deeper moral law of compensation that governed the universe. No
immoral act will long remain without just compensation. Human penal
theories and practices merely echo the natural punishments that await any
sustained immoral actions.

Creativity and growth, as well as death and decay, occur in both
physical and spiritual realms. Any spiritual action, no matter how refined or culturally embedded, will have its strict analogues within the orders of nature. The very power that animates human cultural productivity
derives from the fecund power of a nature that sports diversity and novelty. Human language runs parallel to the inner moral and aesthetic language of nature and merely brings into consciousness that which is
operative throughout a Spirit-governed world. The distortions of contemporary language theory, not to mention those of Continental language mysticism, represent yet one more chapter in the fall from original
revelation that held language properly within the bosom of nature.

In his third proposition (that nature is the symbol of spirit), Emerson
gives voice to the fundamental tenet of his metaphysics. Like Plotinus,
who influenced his writing throughout, Emerson saw the realms of nature as the covering or outer clothing of a presence that was both its origin and goal. As origin, the Spiritual Presence spawned the vitalistic and
indefinitely ramified orders of a world with neither center nor circumference. As goal, the Spirit lures the orders of nature toward a harmony that
will represent the true homecoming of our fragmented state. The Ploti-
nian themes of emanation and return occur in almost all of Emerson's essays, giving voice to his conviction that nature contains within its hidden
core the entire panoply of values and meanings that animate the positive
human religions. Textual condensations of this inner principle and power
merely refract that which should be encountered in purity. The genius/

poet breaks free from textual idolatry to become the finite locus for the volcanic irruption of that which knows no boundary or limit.

If nature is the symbol of spirit, it follows that science, as the systematic and mathematicized analysis of nature, is in the service of the Spirit that operates through natural law. In Emerson's language, "The axioms of physics translate the laws of ethics" (38). This commitment to the convergence of science and human value was reiterated by Peirce and Royce, who insisted that inquiry was evocative of the loyal and agapistic values that animate both the universe and human community. For Emerson, human and cultural value schemes often err in erecting imperatives, such as the Kantian imperative of duty, over the orderly realms of nature, which evidence their own intrinsic values. We need not place our normative life in opposition to nature. Such an imposition represents yet one more stage in the history of the Fall.

Modern science should reinforce the insight into the spiritual foundation of the world. The world itself is a text that becomes open to us through the Spirit of interpretation. As Emerson puts it, "By degrees we may come to know the primitive sense of the permanent objects of nature, so that the world shall be to us an open book, and every form significant of its hidden life and final cause" (40). Form and content both point to the hidden life that speaks to us whenever we allow the currents of Being to break into our willful dealings with the world. As noted, nature has its own language, which represents the *Ursprache,* or depth speech, behind all human utterance. Hermeneutics can recover its original power only when it recognizes that cultural texts derive their power, meaning, and justification from the open book of nature. Contemporary hermeneutics has often looked away from the book of nature and has thereby fueled the relativism and contextualism that has damaged the search for value and Spirit.

Unity has eluded human communities and finite interpreters. What might be called an imperial hermeneutics has celebrated the sheer diversity of perspectives and has, ironically, called into question any unifying movement that would serve to overcome the diremptions that punctuate the human process. Such a hermeneutics is imperial in that it locates validation within the individual and precludes in principle any social or communal articulation of shared meanings. This extreme relativism, often inspired by idiosyncratic readings of Nietzsche and some of his followers, argues that the drive toward unity is in fact a drive toward univocity and dominance. The history of thought is thereby being reread as a history of forms of privileging and domination. To witness to the need for unity is to betray a hidden desire to control and govern perspectives that run counter to one's own perspectival direction and domain.

The issue is not that of preferring unity to difference, as if such a bare choice were meaningful within the structure of the human process. Nor is it that of celebrating sheer plurality, as if that were to guarantee cultural and personal emancipation. Rather, the concern is with keeping the spirits attuned to the unifying power of the Spirit that works in and through the world. Imperial hermeneutics fails to understand the difference between a genuine theonomy, in which autonomy is deepened and secured by the measure of the Divine, and an ever-threatening heteronomy, in which autonomy is broken by the intrusion of an external measure or law. If all theonomous tendencies are mistakenly seen as heteronomous, then it follows that unity is indeed a mere mask for something more sinister and destructive. Only when hermeneutics becomes sensitive to the Spirit, a Presence that can emerge only on the other side of heteronomy, will it overcome its own imperial tendencies.

For Emerson, the drive toward unity is intrinsic to the unfolding of the orders of nature. This unifying telos does not thwart the drive toward creative autonomy but serves, instead, to give its aspirations a proper direction and scope. He states,

> A rule of one art, or a law of one organization, holds throughout nature. So intimate is this Unity, that, it is easily seen, it lies under the undermost garment of nature, and betrays its source in Universal Spirit. . . . It is like a great circle on a sphere, comprising all possible circles; which, however, may be drawn and comprise it in like manner. Every such truth is the absolute Ens (Being) seen from one side. But it has innumerable sides. (49-50)

Unity, and its expression in truth, is analogous to a circle that moves across the surface of a sphere. Of course, such visual similes often distort the deeper categorical insights that they struggle to express. Unity is not merely the spatial encompassment of particular and context-dependent truths. It is more akin to a series of movements that stem from an origin lying just beyond the reach of spatial insight or analysis. These movements ramify and extend into the innumerable subaltern orders of a world that cannot be likened to a sphere adrift in space. Even such a sphere must have a place within which it is located. As we shall see, these spatial images are best left aside when dealing with the concept of the world or of nature as a whole.

Universal Spirit, as the principle and agency of unity within the world, is operative both internally and externally. Emerson occupies a position midway between a theism that would locate the Divine outside of the creation and a pantheism that equates the Divine with the world. His position can be best described as a panentheism. This third perspective locates the Divine both beyond and within the orders of nature. Emerson affirms

> that behind nature, throughout nature, spirit is present; one and not compound it does not act upon us from without, that is, in space and time, but spiritually, or through ourselves: therefore, that spirit is, the Supreme Being, does not build up nature around us but puts it forth through us, as the life of the tree puts forth new branches and leaves through the pores

of the old. As a plant upon the earth, so a man rests upon the bosom of God; he is nourished by unfailing fountains, and draws at his need inexhaustible power. Who can set bounds to the possibilities of man? (67-68)

The Supreme Bring is not to be spatialized in a simplistic manner. Insofar as some spatial analogy is necessary, it is most adequate to state that the divine is found at the font of origin that lies somehow "beneath" the world, while at the same time living as the very sap within the living complexes of nature. Panentheism—strictly, the doctrine that God is both *in* and *beyond* the world—occupies a categorial position that is far more fruitful and open than that occupied by either theism or pantheism. The latter two positions affirm only one dimension of the Divine's complex "spatial" forms of prevalence. Emerson, helped in his analysis by his emphasis on the Spirit, refuses to close off our understanding of the locatedness of the Divine and insists that God qua Spirit is both the power that animates the orders of nature and the inner drive within those orders themselves. Insofar as the Supreme Being puts nature "forth through us," it is correlatively located within our own soul. We need not look to the past or to divine/human figures in order to discover and embrace the Spiritual Presence that quickens our finite existence. Emerson remains bound to the mystical experiences that validated his journey away from the church and rooted him in nature.

Revelation is thus not limited to any finite appearance or text but emerges under the general condition of what might be called a natural grace. Such a grace is prevenient in that it is not actualized by the choices of the human will or earned by specific moral deeds. It is part of the very fabric of Spirit-filled nature and becomes manifest in any creative human act or product. As in some sense prevenient, natural grace quickens the will and points it toward the Divine. Needless to say, such a natural grace is not limited to any given positive religion or sacramental system. The sacraments of the Christian church are mere analogues to the sacramental dimension of the world.

Under the influence of unearned natural grace, we turn away from the idolatry that would locate Spirit in a particular realm or sacred history. In Christological terms, terms not generally used by Emerson, we find that the incarnation is ubiquitous and underlies both human community and the prehuman orders of nature. Insofar as Emerson has a Christology, it can be called a Spirit Christology, in which the third person of the Trinity assumes the dignity and role of the second. Of course, Emerson's Unitarian background precluded speculation of this sort, and he was forced to conflate distinctions that might otherwise operate separately. We come closer to Emerson's intent when we speak of the Spirit-Logos that unifies the diverse orders of creation and lures them toward an eventual convergence in the life of art. The incarnation is rendered articulate in specific works of art that remain translucent to the Spiritual Presence that underlies yet remolds all form. Each complex within nature may, if illuminated from within the light-filled horizon of aesthetic creation, become a locus of the Spirit that works both "beneath" and through nature.

Does it follow that the incarnation is located in every natural complex and order of nature? Is there a sense in which the incarnation may participate in certain complexes and not others? For Emerson, it is clear that the Spirit, the agency of the incarnation, is not equally present in all realities. We may speak of degrees of Spiritual Presence, starting from the least in inert matter moving to the greatest in human genius. By the same token it is clear that a given complex may evolve from a state of spiritual poverty to that of plenitude. It would be most accurate to state that the incarnation is hovering around the edges of things, waiting for appropriate conditions before participating in the inner life of any complex. Nature blooms and decays, waxes and wanes, under the expectation of eventual transformation in the light of the Spirit that remakes and enriches all things.

The measure for each complex comes from the incarnation, which weds matter and Spirit. This binding measure quickens each reality toward the theonomy that stirs at the heart of the world. The radiance of the world emerges through the movement of Spirit in inorganic and organic actualities. It would not be inappropriate to see nature as a community of spirits all underway toward transparency in the Divine. That some things turn away from the Spirit, either through sheer opacity or resistance, gives evidence that the Fall is part of the orders of creation and not confined to human communities. Both prehuman and human configurations are in need of natural grace and the purifying power of the incarnation.

What, then, is the status of the interpretive communities within the orders of nature? Is there a sense in which nature itself is akin to a hermeneutic community? The answer to these questions is crucial in that it attempts to provide the locus for the human enterprise of understanding signs and sign systems. Any hermeneutics that prescinds from the world in which signs are embedded remains unable to explain the natural life histories of bodies of interpretation and to grasp their teleological lure toward convergence and eventual validation. When it is recognized that nature supports and validates sign series and that nature itself is robustly self-interpretive, it becomes easier to explain how human interpretive communities converge on common insights and meanings.

To say that nature interprets itself is not to assert that mind is a trait found throughout the orders of the world. As I noted at the end of chapter 4, idealists from Leibniz to Hartshorne have attempted to solve the problem of the hermeneutics of nature by positing a panpsychism in which each actuality itself is a mind or contains mental operations of a primitive kind. From our perspective, this extends too much metaphysical license toward the human and only reinforces the anthropocentric biases that plague hermeneutic theory. The solution to the problem of natural interpretation must lie elsewhere.

Nature is self-interpreting in a much less dramatic way through the series of prehensions (feelings) that prevail between complexes, whether conscious or not. Insofar as a complex becomes even weakly relevant to another, some change in the trait configuration or scope is manifest. Even if there is no center of consciousness to feel these changes, they are nevertheless prehended in some way and to some degree. By throwing a stone in a pond, a chain of events is started in which the wave patterns are altered and given a new, if short-lived, rhythmic pattern. These wave patterns are possible only because of a prehensive attunement to the novel and intrusive presence of the rock. Insofar as the water surface is altered, we can say, without too much violence to our language, that some sort of rudimentary interpretive process is under way. On the higher levels of animal consciousness, the hermeneutic process becomes more complex. The coloration on a moth serves to warn would-be predators that the given species is visually akin to one that is poisonous. Or consider the fact that a tree under insect invasion can send a warning signal to other trees through releasing particles into the atmosphere. The recipient trees make the obvious and highly compulsive "interpretation" that they must alter their own internal mechanisms if they are to be best prepared for attack. That nature can lie gives striking evidence for the ubiquity of interpretive structures and acts within prehuman orders.

Human interpretive communities, even with their wealth of detail and consciously apprehended sign possibilities, merely deepen interpretive possibilities already slumbering within nature. That Spirit flows across the human/prehuman divide shows that the emergence of a self-conscious human interpreter is not a cosmic mystery but a quickening of the possibilities that represent part of the outward movement of the evolutionary process. Nature itself is an interpretive process through and through—not because it is an alleged series of minds or monads of protoconsciousness but because it prevails as innumerable orders of interaction and evolutionary ramification. From the least complex subatomic particles to the human communities embedded in the Midworld of signs and symbols, the orders of the world struggle toward an increase in hermeneutic success. The so-called struggle for survival is fueled by interpretive acts that work toward either expansion or destruction. Evolutionary competence can be measured in terms of hermeneutic sensitivity. Insofar as an organism prehends the meanings latent within an open situation, it enhances its ability to make suitable adjustments to a condition fraught with tension and danger.

The analogy or metaphor underlying this conception of nature as the ultimate hermeneutic community is that of an endless series of intersecting ellipses with no one central point of convergence. Each ellipse crosses the paths of countless others and becomes sensitive to trajectories not its own. Any given ellipse will have some sense of its own pathway and of that of a number of others. Yet it will never grasp the overall tendency of the entire elliptical universe nor gain access to its contour. It is unclear just what contour nature would have, given that the elliptical intersections have neither center nor circumference. Emerson's circles remain too self-contained, too ready to return to their own point of origin. Ellipses, on the other hand, seem to emerge from a point just beyond the horizon and return to a region equally hidden. Like Peirce's sign series, these ellipses have neither beginning nor end and never attain the kind of self-closure of the circle.

It is not clear that the prehuman orders use signs or sign series, but it is clear that nature is ripe with interpretive transactions. The community of interpretation derives its power and "matter" from the wealth of a world that provides it with interpretive leadings and subsequent forms of validation. If nature is not yet an interpretive community, it is a community of spirits in which membership is largely determined by hermeneutic success. In our conscious struggles to articulate and ramify signs, we are merely working through on a higher level what the orders of nature do without benefit of such conscious sign series. Behind all of our efforts is the Spirit-Interpreter invoked by Royce that lures us toward the interpretive transparency that is the goal of all life. Each gain in our quest for meaning represents an increase of scope for the incarnation that sustains the world.

CONCLUSION:
HERMENEUTICS AND HOPE

In tracing the evolution of American hermeneutics from the transcendental revolution of Emerson, through the pragmatic turn of Peirce and the later Royce, to horizonal hermeneutics, we have touched on several key dimensions of the ethical center of healthy communal life. Chief among these ingredients is the Roycean principle of loyalty to loyalty, which ensures that each finite interpreter remains bound to the process of an open-ended and democratic sign articulation. The loyal interpreter goes beyond his or her particular semiotic possessions in order to ramify and assimilate signs that might lie outside a specific horizon. In this movement beyond the sum of attained signs, some sense of the Encompassing emerges whenever religious symbols become open to that which is neither a human horizon nor another sign. At the very edge of our horizons flickers something that is the true *lux nova* of our ethical life. We will conclude with some reflections on the way of being that keeps loyalty alive and that brings us closer to a nature that itself is in need of redemption.

The primary threat to the community of interpretation is the basic mood of anxiety, crystallized and finitized in specific fears, which hovers around the gateway to nihilism. The oft-cited crisis of nihilism, not an experience for the classical American thinkers, is best understood as the problem of horizonal displacement. Meaning structures become uprooted from their origin in the orders of nature and remain bereft of validation or a meaningful semiotic contour. We can no longer afford the easy confidence of Peirce or Royce and must face into the winds that blow from a far colder region. While thinkers like Heidegger trace the current dilemma of nihilism to the inner logic of the history of Being and its fateful withdrawal in the age of scientific "enframing" and technological manipulation, it is perhaps more judicious to see the current horizonal displacement as the result of the collapse of a genuine eschatological vision.

Anxiety can be defined as the state of attunement that emerges whenever the power of liberating hope is eclipsed by horizonal constriction.

In its movement toward validation, the community of interpretation wields sign systems of unlimited complexity. As we saw in chapter 3, signs can function on six levels, moving from their simple reference to local traits to the symbolic evocation of the Encompassing itself. Within the hermeneutic process, inertia and decay, exacerbated by our fall from natural grace, often weaken the forward initiative of interpreters. Fear of horizonal expansion is as much a part of human nature as hunger for encompassment. Whenever the interpreting community seeks to ground its sign series in merely conventional or ideological structures, it drifts further away from the meaning-filled orders of nature. The optimistic and idealistic perspectives of Emerson, Peirce, and Royce failed to articulate the pervasive drift and sheer uprootedness of the hermeneutic life. While all three thinkers had some sense of the tragic, their overall conceptual attitude was tied to progressivist notions that flourished throughout the nineteenth century. At the same time, however, their conceptual innovations inaugurated a new era in the history of hermeneutic theory and provided the foundations for an understanding that has now become more compelling. We have been arguing throughout that the classical American thinkers created a philosophical hermeneutics that is more powerful and generic than that created in the subsequent period by Continental thinkers.

The human process can be characterized as operating within a polar tension between a sense of finitude and limitation, always showing us our embeddedness in structures of vast power and scope, and a drive for transcendence that is manifest whenever we encounter that which pierces through the outer shells of our horizons. Wisdom consists in the proper balance between these two poles. To overemphasize finitude is to let our sense of limitation blunt our creative and future-oriented drives. To overemphasize transcendence is to ignore the enabling conditions that emerge from the evolutionary process. More important, it make us insensitive to the destructive forces that govern the lives of those who live in heteronomous communities. To balance these twin insights is to live in a world that must experience the power of transcendence in order to remake the finite and historical conditions that reinforce injustice.

The fundamental emotion that overcomes anxiety and its loss of transcendence is hope. Within the opening power of hope, as the eschatological emotion par excellence, the community can derive liberating power that will keep it on the road toward justice and perpetual self-overcoming. Ernst Bloch, who lived on the boundary between atheism and theism, East and West, made this emotion central to his understanding of both nature and history. "Hope, this expectant counter-emotion against anxiety and fear, is therefore the most human of all mental feelings and only accessible to men, and it also refers to the furthest and brightest horizon.

It suits the appetite in the mind which the subject not only has, but of which, as unfulfilled subject, it still essentially consists."[1] Hope keeps horizonal clarity open before our historical consciousness and enables us to overcome the idolatry of any particular horizon. Anxiety is bereft of hope and reinforces the semiotic closure that governs heteronomous communities. The hermeneutic process, no matter how robust or self-conscious, can never free itself from demonic traits as long as it is not animated by the principle of hope. Loyalty to loyalty is possible only under the lure of the eschaton.

The classical American thinkers were aware that the interpretive process best flourished under the guidance of a particular world stance. We saw in some detail how Royce relied on his principle of loyalty as the key to sign articulation. For Peirce, self-control and a frequent flight into interpretive musement (a process that brings us inevitably to reflection on the divine natures) serve as the motor forces for a judicious and expanding analysis of sign systems. Emerson argued for poetic ecstasy as the opening power onto the life of the Spirit that hovers in and around things. In all three cases, some sense of the primacy of the liberating future is evident. Yet the full radicalness of the eschatological perspective was not evident to the classical American thinkers.

The sense of hope can emerge only when we fully grasp the distinction between horizons and the Encompassing. As we argued in chapter 3, the Encompassing is not a perspective or a humanly occupied order that could serve as a horizon of meaning. Horizons are, by definition, realms of finite meaning sustained and concretized by sign series. Each individual interpreter occupies several horizons and learns to translate the semiotic material of one horizon into another. Horizonal fusion and intersection pervade the human process and guarantee at least the rudiments of communal transaction. Standing between particular horizons and the Encompassing is the Midworld, which is more than the mere "sum" of all horizons. The Midworld prevails as the realm within which horizons arise and decay. It points both toward the sheer plurality of horizons and the elusive measure of the Encompassing that limits its own scope. The Midworld makes horizonal fusion possible.

At no point is a given horizon fully transparent, even if its evolving contour can leave traces. These traces are the initial data of the self-conscious hermeneutic process. While no horizon is fully open to the person

---

[1]Ernst Bloch, *The Principle of Hope,* trans. Neville Plaice, Stephen Plaice, and Paul Knight (Cambridge: MIT Press, 1986) 75. In this monumental three-volume work, originally written between 1938 and 1947 in the United States, Bloch lays bare the eschatological principle of human history and argues that it represents the animating core of mythology and religion. This work has become fundamental to Christian-Marxist dialogue.

who occupies it, it is still a reality constituted by given signs and meanings. The Encompassing, on the other hand, has no semiotic wealth—no body of signs that could somehow become available to the individual or community. It stands behind the "sum" of all horizons and serves as the ever-receding Providingness (Buchler) for each horizon. Its most important function is to keep horizons from becoming so self-enclosed that they forget that they are merely finite horizons and that they prevail in a world with other horizons and with that which can never become a mere horizon. The Encompassing lures each horizon beyond its own density toward that light that can never be encompassed or refracted.

Hope is the gift of the Encompassing to us. Insofar as we cling to our horizons, living in forgetfulness of that which transcends all horizons, we are bereft of the liberating hope that keeps us open to world transformation. The fundamental expectant emotion of hope does not affirm specific beliefs about some future state of affairs. Rather, it keeps horizonal expectations attuned to the lure that coaxes each horizon beyond its finite limitations. In Royce's analysis of the Pauline Epistles and the primitive church, the full radicalness of the eschatological principle was ignored. His emphasis shifted to an exhibition of the traits of the body of Christ as the living community of the redeemed. While this focus is not inappropriate, it needs to be gathered into the deeper principle of expectation. Peirce collapsed the principle of hope into a progressive belief in the infinite long run, in which the community of scientific inquirers would arrive at the truth concerning their sign systems. The principle of hope, as understood in terms of Ernst Bloch's redefinition, does not reinforce the progressivist myths that flowered at the end of the nineteenth century. To move from some sense of guaranteed social progress to the power of hope requires a leap across an experiential abyss. Like the leap of faith, the leap of hope breaks free from ideology and horizonal closure. Hope stands as the highest access structure available to interpreters.

Throughout this book, I have been concerned to show how the community of interpretation emerges as one of the key discoveries of American hermeneutic theory. I have attempted to demonstrate that such a community is the horizon within which sign translation takes place. The wealth of the community is found in its innumerable signs, which form into triads of unlimited reach. Neither the beginning nor the end of a series is discoverable by any finite interpreter. At each end lies the eternal mystery of that which is never part of a sign series. This mystery reaches down into the very heart of nature. The recovery of nature, as the Providingness of all signs and meanings, is one of the fundamental tasks of horizonal hermeneutics. The incarnation is slumbering within the mute orders of nature, just as much as it prevails within the realms of the human spirit. Nature's redemption requires a turning within the community of interpreters, a turning that risks the shattering power of the Encompassing so that horizons may become humbled and transformed.

When our horizons are measured by the Encompassing, they in turn become attuned to the interpretive processes within nature that encompass human perspectives and give them direction and validation.

As finite, the community of interpretation remains embedded within sign series that exert their own pressures and have their own lines of convergence. Inertia and historical priority keep signs from derailing into an abyss of chaos and unintelligibility. At the other extreme, the drive toward transcendence keeps the community open to horizonal expansion and the lure of the Encompassing. The gift of hope quickens the life of the community and gives it courage to endure the constraints of finitude. It is not often recognized that no community will have the ability to face its own heteronomous tendencies unless it is grounded in the hope that theonomy remains an ever-present possibility. Without hope, no community will have the power to break free from its interpretive diremptions. Outside the eschatological principle the hermeneutic process is confined to a blind reinforcement of prior forms of domination. Heteronomy and the life of interpretation cannot long live together.

In chapter 3, some of the characteristics of a nonheteronomous community were exhibited. A few further words are in order. The hermeneutic process never exists outside particular political and social structures. The Continental emphasis on the solitary interpreter blunts the movement toward a deeper understanding of the destructive forces that live within the heart of certain communities. Existential hermeneutics has developed a radical autonomy without benefit of a theonomous core. The measure for the individual self remains unable to serve as the measure for social structures. The solipsistic existential hermeneute remains tied to private and highly arbitrary linguistic and textual artifacts. The Continental tradition has therefore been unable to shed light on the social distortions that fragment the community.

The proper political locus for the community of interpretation is in a theonomous democracy in which each individual interpreter is sustained by the power of the Divine, which validates true autonomy while opening it to its proper depth. The perspective defended in this book can prevail only if the forces of heteronomy are shown for what they are—demonic distortions of the hermeneutic process. Paul Tillich, a thinker who, like Ernst Bloch, lived on the boundaries between cultures and ideologies, defined a political vision that keeps hope alive, while attacking heteronomy wherever it appears. In *The Socialist Decision*, Tillich makes eschatology central to the theonomous community.

> Human expectation is always transcendent and immanent at the same time. More precisely, this opposition does not exist for expectation. Any study of prophetic eschatological expectation shows this clearly. The coming order of things is seen in historical continuity with the present; it is immanent. And yet, the concepts used to describe the coming order presuppose

a total transformation of the present, a suspension of the laws of nature. The immanent is in fact transcendent.[2]

The laws of nature are not so much suspended as allowed to show their deeper meaning. Throughout this book it has been suggested that the concept of justice is to be found within the concept of nature and that the unfolding of a just social order is one of the fundamental tasks of the community of interpretation. Tillich's sensitivity to the correlation of hope and justice serves as a reminder of the inseparability of hermeneutics and theonomy.

As horizons become permeable to the Encompassing and as interpreters become open to the theonomous traces in the other, the life of hermeneutics begins to serve the needs of genuine community. The preoccupation with written texts not only has hurt the generic drive of interpretation theory but has thwarted the movement toward communal transformation. Continental hermeneutics, in overemphasizing human texts, has limited our understanding of the objects of interpretation. Pan-textualism not only is impoverished metaphysics but represents a flight from political responsibility. To assert that whatever is, is a text severs the connection between human cultural artifacts and the political and natural orders that sustain or cancel such products. All texts must first be located in a community of interpretation that has broken the hold of heteronomous distortions. Furthermore, these same texts must be shown to belong to the deeper spiritual impulses of nature itself. More encompassing than the sum total of all texts is the unending community of interpretation, which gives all texts their ultimate meaning.

The development of horizonal hermeneutics is concerned with a conceptual and experiential realignment that will secure the community of interpretation against heteronomy from within and without. The life of interpretation is fraught with tension and possible internal breakdown. But it should never be bereft of the liberating hope that is the unearned gift of the Encompassing. In accepting this gift we become foci of hermeneutic renewal and thereby ensure that the incarnation will not be eclipsed by the forces that destroy the Beloved Community.

---

[2]Paul Tillich, *The Socialist Decision,* trans. Franklin Sherman (New York: Harper & Row, 1977) 110. The German text, *Die sozialistische Entscheidung,* was published in 1933. The Nazi government burned all known copies shortly after publication. To this day, this work represents the most important theoretical contribution toward understanding the structures of a theonomous democracy.

• Index of Principal Subjects •

• Index of Names •